Praise for *Anatolian Days and Nights*

"*Anatolian Days and Nights* is an ⬚⬚⬚⬚ ⬚ci-
nating country. Joy Stocke and A⬚ ⬚⬚⬚⬚⬚⬚ ⬚n-
traditions of modern-day Turkey ⬚⬚⬚⬚⬚⬚⬚ of
history at the heart of our human ⬚ ⬚⬚⬚⬚⬚ ...make you want
to grab your bags and hop the next flight to Istanbul."

—**Alan Drew, author of *Gardens of Water***

"In their touching, often humorous memoir, *Anatolian Days and Nights*, Joy Stocke and Angie Brenner write vividly about their journeys through one of the world's most vibrant countries. The landscape and people slip beneath your skin until you are no longer sure whether you've become a part of Turkey or whether Turkey has become a part of you. As a frequent visitor to Turkey, I applaud Stocke and Brenner for skillfully weaving a tale that leaves me yearning to return."

—**Harriet Mayor Fulbright, widow of Senator J. William Fulbright, founder of the Fulbright Program**

"*Anatolian Days and Nights* is a book that feels comfortably familiar, with the authors' explorations starting from the 'safe' territory of a holiday resort and then rippling gently outward. It's a book you can read in an 'I could do that too' frame of mind . . . It succeeds in being thoroughly inspirational."

—**Pat Yale, travel writer, former coauthor of *Lonely Planet Turkey***

"In their vivid memoir, Joy Stocke, a travel writer from New Jersey; and Angie Brenner, a former travel bookstore owner from California, document their travels through Turkey, spanning nearly 10 years and stretching from the Black Sea to the Mediterranean coast, and from the Iranian border to Istanbul . . . Every destination on their itinerary is home to ghosts of Turkey's past, but the friends also take time to enjoy 'whitewashed façades tinged sienna in the late afternoon sun' and 'breezes rustling through the cobbled streets.' Over-eager guides embody the country's tumultuous national identity—a mélange of Muslims, Christians, Jews, Armenians, Turks, and more—and descriptions of the past weaved into the present provide a rich portrait of the region."

—*Publishers Weekly*

"There is a lot to be said for two women, one married with children, the other single, who choose to travel through a country where such a thing provokes shock, distrust, and assumptions about the flexibility of their moral character. The two handle awkward or frightening situations with grace and intelligence."

—*Philadelphia Inquirer*

"The most aromatic book I have ever read, it had me salivating from page one. If you are planning a trip to Turkey, don't leave home without a copy of *Anatolian Days and Nights*. If you're not lucky enough to be going to Turkey, take the tour with Joy and Angie. Read *Anatolian Days and Nights*; it's an exciting, intriguing journey."

—Janet Walker, Bookpleasures.com

"Touching bases with friends who are expatriates to Turkey, hearing various forms of Turkish music (including *harabat*, which could be called the Turkish blues), trying to understand the complications of Turkish politics, and learning to deal with their own yearnings to live in both worlds, the authors continue to struggle to bridge the cultural gap, with visits to Ephesus—said to be the final resting place of Mery-emana, the blessed Virgin Mary, a place of worship and peace—and Yali, a Turkish bar in Kalkan, loud with insistent music and laughter . . . In their explorations, and with quiet times for introspection, they discover that they can embrace all the facets of the people, religion, and culture of Turkey."

—Laura Strathman Hulka, Story Circle Book Reviews

Anatolian
DAYS ☾ & ★ NIGHTS

A Love Affair with Turkey:
Land of Dervishes, Goddesses, and Saints

JOY E. STOCKE & ANGIE BRENNER

ILLUSTRATIONS BY ANGIE BRENNER

Wild River BOOKS

Published by Wild River Books
P.O. Box 53
Stockton, New Jersey 08559
www.wildriverreview.com

Distributed by Emerald Book Company

For ordering information or special discounts for bulk purchases, please contact Emerald Book Company at PO Box 91869, Austin, TX 78709, 512.891.6100.

Design and composition by Greenleaf Book Group LLC
Cover design by Tim Ogline
Watercolors by Angie Brenner

Publisher's Cataloging-In-Publication Data
(Prepared by The Donohue Group, Inc.)
Stocke, Joy E.
  Anatolian days & nights : a love affair with Turkey : land of dervishes, goddesses, and saints / Joy E. Stocke & Angie Brenner ; illustrations by Angie Brenner. — 1st ed.
    p. : ill., maps ; cm.
  Includes bibliographical references and index.
  ISBN: 978-0-9839188-0-6
    1. Turkey—Civilization. 2. Turkey—Description and travel. 3. Stocke, Joy E.—Travel. 4. Brenner, Angie—Travel. 5. Travel books. I. Brenner, Angie. II. Title. III. Title: Anatolian days and nights
DR429.4 .S76 2012
956.1/0411   2011938491

Part of the Tree Neutral® program, which offsets the number of trees consumed in the production and printing of this book by taking proactive steps, such as planting trees in direct proportion to the number of trees used: www.treeneutral.com

Printed in the United States of America on acid-free paper

TreeNeutral®

13 14 15 16 17 18   10 9 8 7 6 5 4 3 2

First Edition

For Jackson.
—AB

For my daughter, Sarah "Sadie" Gretchen Young.
—JES

CONTENTS

AUTHORS' NOTE

Bir varmış bir yokmuş—*maybe it happened,*
maybe it didn't.

—*Turkish proverb*

For nearly twenty years, Turkey has been a part of our lives. For more than ten, we've traveled together, sharing adventures and misadventures. We never found the dangerous country so many Westerners fear. Instead, we discovered a beautiful, vibrant, diverse culture as complicated as our own.

We've chosen to use the word Anatolia, Land of Many Mothers, in our title, derived from *Anat*, the great mother goddess. Within Anatolia's borders we've visited places we read about in history books, the Bible, and in myth: Mesopotamia, the Pontus, Cappadocia, and the Fertile Crescent.

But it was through author Mary Lee Settle's writings that we first came across the phrase *Bir varmış bir yokmuş*—maybe it happened, maybe it didn't. Throughout our journeys, the phrase has stayed in our minds.

Reality is framed within our memories. Maybe it happened, but then again . . .

TURKISH PRONUNCIATION

c	j sound as in *j*am
ç	ch sound as in *ch*urch
g	as in *g*o when before or after vowels: a, ı, o, u
g	as in ang*u*lar when before or after vowels: e, i, ö, ü
ğ	lengthens the vowel sound, almost not heard, like nei*gh*bor
ı	like u in meas*u*re
i	as in b*ee*t
j	as in plea*s*ure
o	as in t*o*ne or *o*re
ö	like ur in f*ur*
ş	sh sound as in *sh*oot
u	as in b*u*ll
ü	as u in pl*u*me, like French t*u*

Diphthongs

ay	like igh in s*igh*t
ey	like ay in s*ay*
oy	like oy in *c*oy

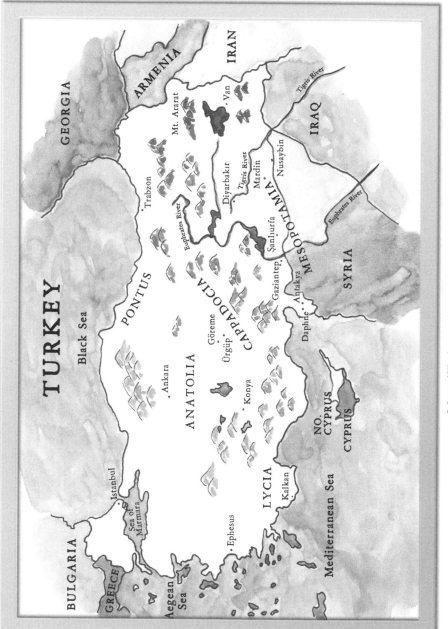

Map of Turkey and surrounding area

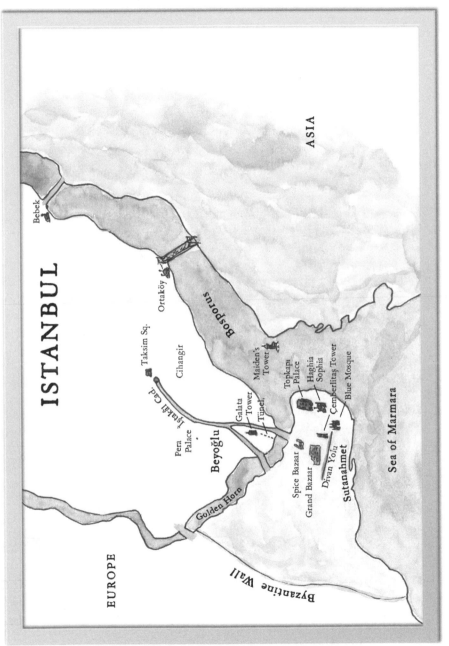

Map of Istanbul and surrounding area

PROLOGUE

How easy it is to fall in love with Turkey's Mediterranean coast. Light shines from sea to rock in elusive reflections. Pine-covered cliffs reveal fissures and coves where fragrant boughs brush against water. From a plateau rises a 4,000-year-old village of tombs, all that remains of the goddess-worshipping Lycians who settled in the fertile, protected valleys.

Today, our boat shelters in a bay where Phoenician traders once dropped anchor, and where we find the ruins of an ancient city glimmering beneath turquoise water. We climb over rocks onto the shore and see a girl standing in a grove of olive trees. Her hair is wrapped in a scarf edged with tiny shells and tied at the crown of her head.

She gathers olives that have fallen to the ground and studies us, two women in sunglasses, tank tops, shorts, and hiking boots. Gravely, she places a handful of the bitter, green fruit on a stone ledge, an offering. And darts away.

INTRODUCTION

Anatolia:

From the Greek word meaning East—the land of the rising sun. Once the name of Asia Minor, today Anatolia refers to the country called Turkey, whose borders stretch from the Balkans to Armenia, Georgia, Iran, Iraq, and Syria.

Joy

On a morning in early May 2007 in the foothills of the Kaçkar Mountains on the eastern spur of the Silk Road, Angie and I climb the steps of an abandoned Orthodox Christian church.

We hear a whoosh. The flutter of wings. Doves swoop through the fragile remains of arches and walls, their wings radiating sunlight as they circle a high dome where a serene Madonna gazes at us with almond-shaped eyes, her son enveloped within the folds of a sky-blue cloak.

So convinced are we that we've been given a glimpse of heaven, we forget to factor in the law of balance. An hour later, the universe rights itself. On a deserted stretch of highway heading east toward the city of Van, a loud bang shakes the engine of our rental car.

I glance at Angie, whose furrowed brow reflects the sinking feeling in my gut. Perhaps we'd pushed the tiny Czech Škoda to its limits when we climbed the steep, rutted incline to the monastery. "It should have been up to the task," I say, as I maneuver the Škoda to the side of the road.

In answer to our anxiety, the engine hisses an oily plume of smoke and shudders a death rattle.

Angie opens her door and steps into a hot afternoon. On both sides of the road, green and dun-colored grasses undulate toward the horizon. Not a single car or truck passes by. Except for the cicadas chirring in the trees, we seem to be the only living creatures in eastern Anatolia.

I release the hood and Angie gingerly lifts it. An acrid wisp of smoke fades into the air.

"We're going to need help," she says, shielding her eyes and scanning the empty road.

I try my cell phone, but it's had no reception since we reached the Kaçkar Mountains.

We had seen a farmhouse about a mile behind us and, near it, a man working in an apple orchard. Our dread easing, we grab our backpacks, lock the car doors, and set out for the farmhouse.

The sun blazes against the blue sky. Sweat collects in the hollows of our backs. When we reach the farmhouse, we see the man sitting on a vine-covered porch, a gray and black Anatolian shepherd dog the size of a pony by his side. He almost smiles as he takes in the spectacle of two women walking toward him, me in hiking boots, a floppy beige garden hat, and khaki shorts, and Angie in leather sandals she purchased days earlier in Istanbul's Grand Bazaar. A green linen sundress brushes her ankles; her hair is pulled back in a silver clip beneath a sun visor.

The dog bares his teeth and growls.

"*Merhaba*. Hello," calls the man.

"Merhaba," says Angie. She gestures toward our car, now a steamy mirage on the horizon. "Auto kaput."

The man beckons us past the growling dog, up wooden steps and through a heavy wooden door. We enter a small kitchen with a half fridge, propane stove, and porcelain sink set into a beige linoleum counter beneath a window that looks out to the road.

His wife turns from the sink. She wears a red cotton headscarf patterned with blue and yellow flowers and voluminous *shalwar* pants pleated at her ankles. She takes a crinkled apple from a plastic bowl and sets it on a cutting board.

"*Hoşgeldiniz*. Welcome," she says, smiling as if she's been expecting us.

The man speaks quietly while she slices the apple and arranges it on a white plastic plate. After setting the plate and a jar of honey on the table and urging us to sit and eat, she makes tea, pours it into three tulip-shaped glasses, and sends her husband down the steps toward the road, his dog trailing behind him.

"*Benim arkadaşlarım*, my friends," she says, and touches her belly, asking questions in Turkish about children, spouses, and our homes, which we answer in English. Somehow it works.

Later, clucking his tongue and looking as if one of our closest relatives has died, the man trudges back up the steps.

"*Evet*, yes," he says, looking at me with sorrowful eyes. "*Auto* kaput."

I hand him the business card from the rental agency in Erzurum, a hundred miles away.

"We had a bad feeling about that company," Angie says to the wife, who takes Angie's hand between her palms. "We should have used the agency in our hotel, but one of our friends recommended this one so we could save money."

At seventy-five dollars a day, it was hardly a bargain, I think.

The man beckons us to the window. On the road a flatbed truck idles, its red cab swirled with yellow and white flowers.

Three men brace themselves on the truck bed behind our poor little Škoda, securing the Škoda's wheels with twine for the long haul back to Erzurum.

Painted in white across the truck's bumper are the words: *Maşaallah*, Whatever God Wills.

Angie and I didn't plan to fall in love with Turkey. We often say that Turkey's history, beautiful coast, and superb cuisine keep luring us back. True, but how do we explain the subtleties of a culture that overwhelmed our senses, one moment leaving us delighted and the next leaving us ready to pack our bags and take the first flight home? How to explain chance encounters that turn into devoted friendships?

Yet our love for Turkey sprang from a more conventional kind of love, the love of a woman for a man. Or, more specifically, our friend Wendy's love affair with a Turkish man.

Wendy, a travel specialist, and I had been friends since our twenties. I had written the first brochures for her business specializing in travel to Greece and Turkey. On New Year's Eve heading into 2000, my husband and I celebrated the coming millennium with Wendy and her boyfriend, a Greek man named Dimitri, of whom I was very fond. That night, she made a resolution to sell her business and move with Dimitri to the Greek island of Santorini, where he had a hotel.

Now, in the spring of 2001, she had broken up with Dimitri and fallen in love with a Turkish man named Orhan. With her money, she and Orhan had leased a guesthouse and a restaurant in a former Greek fishing village called Kalkan on Turkey's Mediterranean coast.

When I asked why she chose Turkey instead of our beloved Greece, she assured me she was deeply in love with Orhan and that Kalkan would remind me of the small village we had visited fifteen years before on the Greek island of Kos.

I remembered taking a ferry on a day trip from Kos to the resort town of Bodrum on the Turkish coast. We had bought cinnamon sticks and pistachios in an outdoor bazaar near the harbor and had watched an old man who, for twenty dollars, took Polaroid pictures of tourists sitting nervously atop his ancient camel.

"I'm happy to settle in Turkey," Wendy had said. "Besides, Greece has become too expensive."

While she closed her business in the States, she asked Angie and me to help Orhan run the pension for the summer. Although Angie and I were perfect strangers, Wendy assured each of us that we would become friends.

Two months later, Angie and I found ourselves on the creaky balcony of Wendy's pension overlooking the harbor of Kalkan, Turkey, sharing a bottle of wine. By the time we finished our first glass, we discovered that we had much in common. We had been raised in the Midwest, on the shores of Lake Michigan—Angie in Michigan, I in Wisconsin.

I confessed that I had been filled with wanderlust since I was a child. I had spent many afternoons hiking the bluffs near my house and watching steamers travel north toward the Saint Lawrence Seaway and the Atlantic Ocean, imagining myself on them.

"I felt the same way," said Angie, smiling in recognition, "the longing to jump on a ship and go."

I told her that my grandmother and grandfather had left eastern Germany in the 1920s, during the last years of the Weimar Republic. As a series of strokes unmoored my grandmother's mind from the present, she would talk about her childhood, how on Sundays she had danced with friends in the beer garden of her village near Berlin. About how she had longed for adventure and finally found it on a ship that brought her from Bremerhaven to New York.

On a night midway across the Atlantic, the ship's captain invited her to sit at his table for dinner. "I wore a pink silk dress with pin tucks on the bodice. My sister sewed it for me as a going-away present," she said, her watery eyes taking on a dreamy quality. "And the captain, he was so handsome in his blue jacket. When the band played *The Blue Danube* waltz, he asked me to dance."

In her manner and humor, my grandmother possessed a gentility I found again in Turkey.

Angie dreamed of traveling to places she discovered in her father's *National Geographic* magazines and pretended the civilizations she saw in the photographs existed on the other side of the lake.

"My father always wanted to see the world," she had said. "But he never had the courage to live the life he wanted, so in some ways I'm living his dream."

Later, she brought the stories she read to life by traveling among the Hmong people in Vietnam, to the Islamic island of Zanzibar in the Indian Ocean, and to the Maasai Mara of East Africa. She sought tribal cultures with rituals and communal lives long forgotten in the West.

We left the Midwest as teenagers. Angie went to the West Coast and became part of the first generation of women in corporate management. Eventually she walked away to fulfill her dream of owning a travel bookstore. I went to the East Coast, married my college sweetheart, had a daughter, and began a career reviewing hotels in Greece and Italy for a travel company. My husband, Fred, had begun his own career in banking, and because childcare was hard to find, I often brought our daughter, Sarah, with me.

As Angie's and my friendship grew, Turkey became the most seductive of suitors: intriguing and conflicted, with a conservative eastern border and a hedonistic Mediterranean coast where tourists tan topless and dance in discos until wisps of hot-pink clouds hint at the coming of dawn.

When we returned home, friends and family breathed a sigh of relief and said, "You're not going back; it's too dangerous."

Yet, how do we explain Turkish hospitality, which has sheltered and protected us in the smallest villages as well as the chicest Istanbul apartments? How to describe the apartment overlooking the Bosporus where Sephardic Jewish friends serve tea with nuts and sweets, and conversation flows in Turkish, English, German, and Russian? Or the carpet seller in Cappadocia who, at lunchtime, puts his carpets aside and thinks nothing of offering his customers lamb stew his mother made?

At times Angie and I have thought that maybe it's better not to change anyone's mind, that we should keep beautiful and complicated Turkey to ourselves.

But that would be a betrayal.

Spring

2001

Chapter One

LYCIAN DAYS

By the time the wise woman has found a bridge,
the crazy woman has crossed the water.

—*Turkish proverb*

Angie

Kalkan's elegant houses perch on a hillside in a half-moon cove above the Mediterranean Sea, their whitewashed façades tinged sienna in the late afternoon sun. A breeze rustles through the cobbled streets in anticipation of cocktail hour, but my only thought is to find the Sun Pension, owned by my friend Wendy and her boyfriend, Orhan.

The scent of spiced, grilled meat wafts in the air, and my stomach growls. After traveling twenty-four hours on planes and buses, I'm exhausted, hungry, and disappointed. When I arrived at the airport in Istanbul, I called Orhan, who said he'd be here to greet me. At least that's what I thought he said.

I had met him the year before, when Wendy invited him to the States. While he spoke little English and I spoke even less Turkish, he seemed pleasant enough. Now, still half expecting him to appear, out of breath and full of apologies, I hire a taxi and watch the driver heave my bags into the trunk.

Among T-shirts, sundresses, shorts, and bathing suits, I've packed the extra linens and cooking utensils Wendy requested, ten pounds of coffee beans, and recipes for gourmet breakfasts—all the items I'll need to host guests in Wendy's boutique pension while Orhan opens their new seaside restaurant.

"And you'll finally meet Joy," Wendy had said, referring to her friend who lived in New Jersey.

I was eager to meet Joy, a writer who had managed to combine her career with marriage and motherhood. For ten years, she had been traveling through Greece, often with Wendy and many times with her daughter, learning the language and writing about the threads of religion that crisscrossed the country.

"She's interested in following those threads through Turkey," Wendy had told me.

The opportunity to manage the Sun Pension had come at the perfect time. I had recently closed my travel bookstore, which left me emotionally and financially depleted. It didn't take much arm-twisting on Wendy's part to persuade me to go. Instead of reading about women who took off and lived in other countries, I would be the one sitting by the sea and writing my own stories. Joy and I would fix sumptuous breakfasts for our guests; straighten rooms, adding small personal touches; and then retire to the balcony of the Sun Pension, where we would talk about books. And I would start my writing career.

Besides, I had been in Kalkan once before, with my former boyfriend, Sami, a businessman from Istanbul. I'd met him nearly four years earlier on a minibus traveling along the Mediterranean coast from Antalya to Kaş. For over three years, we kept up our long-distance relationship by flying between Istanbul and San Diego. While I ran my all-consuming bookstore, Sami attempted to open an import business in the States. The red tape of starting a business proved difficult, and he was equally frustrated with opinions Americans often have about Turkey: that it's a dangerous country filled with Muslim fanatics.

Even more difficult for him was the lack of a café life in the Southern California suburbs. Sami missed the social bonds he had in Istanbul, where friends gathered regularly for coffee or tea and to play backgammon and discuss politics. At times he settled into depression. While I worked, he would sit for hours in my living room or outside the bookstore, chain-smoking Marlboros, wishing he were back in Istanbul—at least until it was time for dinner.

I never met anyone who so enthusiastically excelled at dining out. Like a sultan holding court, he reveled in the pleasure of a perfectly roasted chicken and creamy morel mushrooms while he told me tales of his life in Istanbul. This was when I loved him most, and I became an eager pupil of all things Turkish. He taught me the nuances of language, how to gently press the tip of my tongue against the roof of my mouth to create a gentle rolling of the *r* when I said merhaba, hello.

"To learn a tongue, you must touch a tongue," he would say. He also shared the intimate culinary secrets of his country: which regions have the best shish kebab and which restaurants in those regions have the flakiest baklava the creamiest yogurt.

I memorized idioms that would mark me as a local and learned the subtleties of Ottoman politesse in everyday greetings. For instance, when I visited his family, he taught me that it is important to pay homage to the oldest male relative before greeting anyone else.

"Close your business, marry me, and we will live in Istanbul," was his halfhearted suggestion before he finally left California for Turkey. But he had shown me another side of Turkish culture that made me wary.

He was the firstborn and only son, an honored position among all classes in Turkey. When I visited him in Istanbul, he came and went without answering to anyone. And when I asked where he was going, he would shrug his shoulders, indicating that the question was too trivial to answer. I knew he wasn't trying to be rude or evasive, but I began to question my self-worth, wondering when he would disappear again and leave me for hours in his family's Istanbul apartment with his mother who spoke no English.

It became painfully clear that Sami and I weren't ready to tackle the cultural gap, nor was I ready to throw in the towel with my bookstore. We parted as friends, but after Sami left, I realized I was still in love with his country.

The taxi stops at a dead-end alley piled with dirt and broken concrete, behind a small grocery store.

"*Lütfen*. Please," I say. "I'm looking for the Sun Pension."

At first I think the driver misunderstands when he points to a dilapidated building with a tilting balcony barely holding up fist-thick vines of tangled magenta bougainvillea.

He removes my bags from the trunk and sets them in the dirt.

"Evet," he says. "Yes. The Sun Pension is here."

He carries the bags across a wooden plank straddling a pool of mud.

The percussive sound of a jackhammer rattles the street. A shadow crosses the driver's face when he sees my distress. Over glasses of wine and plates of olives and cheese in my bookstore, Wendy had described the beautiful sea view from the pension's balcony, the Turkish cotton towels hand-embroidered with colorful fish, vases and soap dishes from a pottery factory in Kütahya. But she had neglected to tell me that next door, workmen were gutting and rebuilding one of the town's long-abandoned Greek mansions.

In the nineteenth century, at the invitation of the Ottoman Empire, Kalkan welcomed a wealthy class of Greek shipping merchants. This particular mansion looks as if it's been empty since the owners were forced to leave during the 1923 population exchange between Turkey and Greece.

The voices of squabbling children and a baby's cry drift from the alley. The driver lugs my bags up a rickety set of stairs and sets them on a small landing.

This can't be the pension Wendy described, I think, as I open the door to a dingy entrance where a bare overhead bulb sheds light on a scarred, wooden desk. But sure enough, Wendy's business card is tucked beneath a blue and white floral ashtray overflowing with cigarette butts.

"Orhan?" I call.

A block of white cheese sits on a cutting board near a small sink in an alcove off the entrance. Except for the ashtray, the cheese, and a rather large cockroach perched on the counter, one could think the pension has been abandoned. Exhausted, I watch the cockroach scuttle across the cheese and disappear down the sink's drain.

I throw away the cheese and wipe down the counter before carefully opening the first of five doors, all with keys in their locks. Inside I find a small, pine-paneled room with twin beds covered in white bedspreads and separated by a wooden nightstand. The bathroom barely contains a pull-chain toilet, chipped porcelain sink, and handheld shower with a drain in the center of the floor.

After hanging my toiletry bag on the bathroom door, I strip off the clothes I've worn for twenty-four hours and turn on the shower taps. Pipes rumble and creak. A trickle of rusty water drips from the showerhead. From a cotton washcloth draped over the edge of the sink, an embroidered blue-eyed, hot-pink fish seems to mock me with bright red lips. I grab him by the tail and clean off the road dust as best I can.

I put on my pajamas and robe and venture back into the lobby.

It's noon in California, a good time to reach Wendy, I think. I sit at the desk, pick up the telephone receiver, and dial Wendy's number. In the middle of the first ring, her voicemail picks up. "Your message is important to me," says an upbeat Wendy. "Please leave it at the beep."

"I'm here," I say, my voice betraying my frustration. "But I can't find Orhan. Call me as soon as you get this."

I hang up and impulsively dial the Istanbul telephone number I know by heart. It's been several months since I've spoken with Sami.

"*Ahlo!*" says the familiar voice.

"Sami?" I say.

"Ahngeee!" he shouts into the receiver. "Where are you? What are you doing? Are you in Istanbul?"

The enthusiasm in his cigarette-roughened voice makes me wish that I *were* in Istanbul. I hesitate before answering his questions. So much has happened since he left San Diego and moved back to Istanbul. I want to tell him how strange it feels to be in Turkey without him, that maybe our breakup happened too fast.

"I'm in Kalkan to run Wendy's pension," I say, and explain that it's not the boutique hotel Wendy had described.

"Ah, Wendy," he says. He had met her on several occasions when she gave presentations at my bookstore. "Yes, she is fun, but she is always a problem."

I hate to admit that he's right. There were problems with Wendy. For one, she often showed up nearly an hour late for scheduled talks at my bookstore, but always with armloads of cheese, wine, and olives. And because she was charming and funny, everyone forgave her.

Like me, she was a single woman in her forties who devoted long hours to her business. She was also a risk taker and shared my love of travel. Her decision to settle down with Orhan was one I could have made with Sami.

"You must leave this place," says Sami. "Come to Istanbul."

A sense of relief rushes through me. His familiar voice and decisive attitude are just what I need. I imagine leaning against his shoulder, smelling his elegant cologne. Is he offering me another chance?

While I consider myself to be an independent businesswoman, I also realize how much I relied on the intimacy between us. Sami's strong opinions and ideas of what I should do were often a source of frustration, but they also showed he was very much a presence in my life.

I begin to fantasize that tomorrow I'll fly to Istanbul. He'll pick me up at the airport and take me to a taverna along the Bosporus where we'll drink glasses of Turkish *rakı* and watch the sun set in a hazy peach glow. This time, without the business to tie me down, things will be different.

I pause, then ask the question whose answer I dread.

"Yes, I am seeing someone," he says. "She's OK." His voice trails off.

That's when it hits me. In the deepest corner of my heart, I've kindled hope for reconciliation. The flame sputters out. I won't fly to Istanbul. He won't pick me up at the airport. I'll have to figure this out myself. I hang up the phone after promising to call if I need anything.

Loneliness shifts to resolve. I unpack the coffee and my French press, ready to face my new life.

Later, beneath thin cotton sheets, my mind drifts to Wendy's friend Joy. How will she react to the pension, I wonder. If I can barely make it through a few hours, how will we get through the summer? And where's Orhan?

The drone of a tenacious mosquito buzzes in my ear, and then I fall into a deep sleep.

A week later, after meeting Orhan, who, except for drinking my coffee, has chosen to ignore me, and after a frustrating call from Wendy, who asks me to be patient with Orhan, I watch a woman heft a large suitcase over the dirt in the alley. She sets down the bag, slips her backpack to the ground, and props her cat's-eye sunglasses on her head. A bewildered expression crosses her face.

"Are you looking for the Sun Pension?" I shout from the balcony over the pounding of hammers next door.

She shields her eyes. "Angie?" she asks, her voice uncertain.

I hold up my glass of wine. It glints as pale as the watery sunlight filtering into the alley. "Welcome to the Sun Pension," I say, forcing a smile. "You must be Joy."

She picks up the pack, lugs the suitcase up the back steps, and drops the bags in a corner of the lobby. I'm petite and just over five feet, and she's nearly a foot taller and athletically built, dressed in straight-leg jeans, black tank top, and a worn jean jacket. Her face is open and friendly, set off by wide cheekbones, dimples, and blue-green eyes that narrow as she takes in the surroundings. I notice her forehead crease with the same combination of exhaustion, anger, and shock I felt a week earlier.

"I could use a glass of whatever you're drinking," she says, regaining a measure of composure and glancing toward the ceiling, where cobwebs float like abandoned clouds. She slumps into a chair next to the lobby desk and loosens the laces of her hiking boots.

I rummage through the kitchen shelf, find a wineglass, fill it, and hand it to her.

"At least Wendy was right when she said I would fall in love with the bougainvillea," says Joy, clinking my glass before taking a sip of her wine. "I've never seen such an abundant display of magenta, which is how I knew I was in the right place."

She pauses and tilts her head as if she's looking for something she can't quite see. "Honestly, this isn't like Wendy at all. Last summer, we reviewed hotels in Capri and Positano. I didn't expect the pension to be a palazzo, but I imagined a charming place with colorful carpets and a brass table or two, set for tea. What was she thinking?"

"About Orhan," I answer. "She's always managed to keep her personal life separate from business. Except this time."

"I didn't give him much thought at all," says Joy with a slight smile. "I was so eager to be here."

Sensing an equal measure of irony and humor in her voice, I relax for the first time in a week.

At sunset, we settle into chairs on the balcony, with its travel-brochure view of a half-moon harbor where gleaming yachts and small pleasure boats rock on gentle waves. For more than two hours, we sort out how and why we are sitting in this ragtag hostel.

"When Wendy and I met in our early twenties, neither of us had been outside the States," says Joy. "On our first trip abroad, we landed in Athens and later found ourselves on the Dodecanese island of Kos, tucked into the Turkish coast. The moment we stepped into the Aegean light, we felt as if we had returned to a home we knew in our souls. I fell in love with the sea, the language, and the way myth was woven into everyday life. I had a fisherman friend who took me out in his boat to a cove where he said I would meet his friend, a mermaid." She smiles. "Although I never saw her, I still half believe she was just beneath the waves."

Joy describes how shortly after her first trip to Greece, she married her college sweetheart, Fred, and had a daughter, Sarah.

"I helped Wendy start her travel business," she continues. "Although Fred couldn't quite understand my obsession with the Mediterranean, he didn't interfere with my travels as long as I brought Sarah, which was easy. The Greek grandmothers love their babies and treated Sarah as one of their own. They were as loving to her as my own grandmother was to me, looking after her, feeding her powdered-sugar cookies, and calling her *koukla-mou*, my little doll."

Then Joy shares how an experience on the island of Crete, in the southern Mediterranean, pushed her to travel farther into Anatolia.

"I hiked to a cave called *h Spilia tis Arkoudas*, the Cave of the Bear. At its entrance was a shrine filled with votive candles and offerings to the Virgin Mary. But when I ventured further inside, in the dank shadows I saw a six-foot-tall stalagmite bear. The local priest told me that worshippers had come to the cave since the time of the Minoan civilization, more than three thousand years ago. I have never before or since experienced what I can only call a pulsing of energy, as if all the voices and the prayers still echoed from the walls. Later I learned that the bear had long been associated with the great mother goddess, Artemis. She was still worshipped just across the Aegean at Ephesus in Turkey when the apostle Paul made his journeys. I remembered Paul's Letters to the Ephesians from Sunday sermons, but the priests never mentioned the scope of her influence in the ancient world."

Joy holds the bowl of her wineglass in her palms and measures her words. "When Sarah was small, it was easier to bring her with me. Now that she's older, it's hard to balance her school schedule with Fred's work schedule and my work and travel schedules. Truth is, I need both worlds: one where I'm compelled to follow the clues in caves and museums and language as if they're songlines, and another at home, where there are school plays and dances and bake sales and parent-teacher conferences. I was hoping to bring my family and some friends to the pension next year."

She leans her chair against the wall and away from the sloping balcony. "But I couldn't have them stay here."

I look at the scratched floors in the hallway and at the bougain-villea vines and can't decide if they are pulling the balcony down or holding it up.

Although I've never been married or had children, I appreciate Joy's challenge of juggling schedules and admire her for wanting to share her dream with family and friends. For Wendy and me, single women who have devoted long hours to our businesses, it's been difficult to sustain romantic relationships. Men are often attracted to us for our business skills and independence, but there comes a point when they expect us to devote less time to our businesses and more time to them.

"I understand Wendy's desire to settle down with Orhan," I say.

"It's a subject she and I have spent hours discussing and one of the reasons we became friends. She's always wanted to combine her tour business in the Mediterranean with a personal life. A few years ago, I came close to realizing Wendy's dream and almost married my Turkish boyfriend Sami. We thought about buying a *gulet*—a Turkish sailing yacht—and starting a small tour business near Kalkan. But I had to run my bookstore and wasn't ready to give it up, at least not then. Plus, Sami was supporting an ex-wife and daughter. Although he came from a sophisticated, secular family who rejected anything to do with fundamentalism, there were signs early on that we were in the midst of a cultural gap."

I pause, wondering if I've shared too much, but Joy's face is filled with compassion, and so I continue. "He was used to doing what he pleased," I say. "He asked me to close my business, marry him, and move to Istanbul, but my heart told me not to do it. I loved him and his beautiful city, but I was afraid I'd be trapped and lonely. When Wendy told me she had rented the pension with Orhan, I had a moment of regret that I didn't say yes. To this day, I wonder what my life might have been like."

Joy gazes across Kalkan Harbor. The horizon has condensed into deep mauve. A band of white light separates water from sky.

"I had a Greek lover long ago," she smiles. "He viewed me more as a possession than a partner, but the intensity was seductive, and it was from him that I first learned how to read the Greek alphabet on a black manual typewriter. Like you, I've thought about the life I might have lived along the Mediterranean Sea."

"It seems that Wendy's not the only one wanting to live in a dream world. But I think this time she's allowed her romantic dream to cloud her judgment," I say, bringing us back to the topic of Orhan and the pension. "I've barely seen him, although a few days ago he invited me for a drink at Lipsos Bar on the eastern edge of the harbor. After introducing his friend Habib, a local hotel owner from Istanbul, Orhan left me sitting at the bar. It felt awkward."

I run my fingertip along the lip of my glass. "Orhan seldom comes home before dawn. And then there are midnight phone calls from a whiskey-voiced woman asking to *speeeak* to *Orrrhan*. I called Wendy, but she didn't want to hear about it."

"You can't blame her," says Joy. "She's sunk all her money into the pension and Orhan's restaurant."

My frustration crystallizes into anger. "Then let's try to salvage this situation."

The following morning, coffee cups in hand, Joy and I lean over the balcony. "There are some advantages to the pension," I whisper, and motion Joy to look over the rail into the courtyard of the mansion next door.

Unaware of our presence, the workmen strip off leather jackets, dress shirts, and trousers, down to their underwear. But this is no ordinary underwear, no boxers or white Fruit of the Looms. They wear tight, colorful Speedo briefs, flashing muscular torsos before slipping into concrete-splattered coveralls.

Seven days a week, after the morning call to prayer, the men arrive in a flatbed truck, reminding me of Byzantine icons with their jet-black hair and almond-shaped eyes. I've learned they're part of Turkey's largest ethnic minority, Kurds, and from Lake Van, near the Iranian border. Years of civil war between the Turkish government and the Kurds have left a legacy of spilled blood and mistrust. With the capture and imprisonment of Abdullah Öcalan, accused terrorist and self-appointed leader of the Kurdish Workers Party, PKK, and with the government's agreement to let Kurds speak their own language, the country holds on to a tenuous peace.

The men laugh and joke, looking charmingly innocent, hardly the dangerous terrorists often portrayed in the media.

"Have you been to eastern Turkey?" asks Joy, sipping her coffee.

"Only as far as Nemrut Dagi, near the Atatürk Dam, on a two-day tour from Cappadocia," I say. "But I've wanted to go farther east, especially to Mardin, where Syrian Orthodox Christians still speak Aramaic, the language of Jesus."

Joy tilts her head as if she sees something hovering on the horizon. "In Urfa, which isn't far from Mardin, there's a Phoenician river goddess I've been reading about called Atargatis. She took the form of a mermaid and is associated with the Virgin Mary."

"Why don't we go?" I say, recognizing a mutual sense of wanderlust.

As the days pass and the work next door progresses, we become friendly with the workmen—who rarely mix with the locals—bringing them coffee in the morning. In return, they've built a small wooden bridge over the dirt in the alley. The neighbors are as suspicious of us as they are of the workmen. Not exactly locals or tourists, we've become a source of curiosity. Shopkeepers, hoping to make a sale, call out when we pass by, inviting us in for tulip-shaped glasses of tea.

At first, we accept most invitations, carefully answering their questions. "Why are you here? Are you married? Does your husband let you travel alone? Are you spying on Orhan for Wendy?"

"No, we're here only to run the pension so Orhan can open his restaurant," we say, which does little to squelch their curiosity.

After too many glasses of tea and tiresome questions, we avoid them, slipping through the narrow lanes and alternating our routes to the pension, heads down, hats pulled over our eyes. Our evasiveness makes the shopkeepers only more inquisitive.

"*La ilaha Illa 'Llah*—There is no god but God."

The call to prayer vibrates through lanes and alleys and expands toward the harbor. Men in dark, baggy trousers and skullcaps walk to the mosque, while Nusrat, owner of Lipsos Bar, opens the evening's first bottle of rakı, the licorice-flavored national drink of Turkey.

When Joy and I take seats at one end of the horseshoe-shaped bar, Nusrat greets us with cheek kisses and a small copper bowl filled with dried, salted chickpeas. From across the bar, Bekir, who owns an antique shop in the center of town, and Doğan, who has a silver shop on the main street, wave hello.

All eyes shift to Habib, the hotel owner I'd met through Orhan. Dressed in khaki pants and a white linen shirt with a soft sweater draped over his shoulders, thick salt-and-pepper hair slightly tousled, he strolls in with an air of confident nonchalance I remember so fondly from my years with Sami. After another round of cheek kisses, he slides onto a stool next to me. His lemon-scented cologne lingers in the humid air.

Immediately, Nusrat draws him into a heated conversation with Bekir and Doğan.

Habib shouts something at Bekir, who turns to Doğan, who shouts something at Nusrat. Soon they're talking at the same time, slapping rakı glasses on the bar.

Just when we're convinced they'll come to blows, Habib rests his hand on my arm. "Don't worry, *canım*, my dear," he says. "We are only talking about fish. You see, there is a special way of baking a whole fish in salt, but we disagree on the type and the coarseness of the salt. We all think the best recipes come from the region where we were born. And since I was born in Izmir, near the Aegean Sea, there is no fish better than grilled red mullet stuffed with fresh dill. You must try it."

"*Hayir*, no," says Bekir. "You must first coat the fish in red pepper paste, as we do in Gaziantep."

Not to be left out, Doğan explains that his favorite fish, *hamsi*, sardines, is best coated in corn meal and deep-fried in sunflower oil.

"Don't listen to him," says Bekir. "He's Laz," referring to the Laz people, who live in the Black Sea region and who, like people of Polish ancestry in the States, are often the butt of jokes.

"The Laz people have more than a thousand ways to cook hamsi," says Doğan. "Everyone loves fried hamsi."

"It's all *geyik muhabetti*," says Nusrat, to much laughter.

Noticing our confusion, Habib explains, "It literally means deer chat. To talk and say nothing, like a herd of deer in a field. It makes no sense, but that's the point."

With his eyes fixed on mine, he brings his glass to full, soft lips.

I'm beginning to see why Habib's friends are drawn to him. Already I'm seduced by his quick wit and sexy intensity.

When the conversation about fish wears itself out, talk turns to the pension.

"Orhan was a bartender when he met Wendy," says Habib. "He knows nothing about the restaurant business."

"He's a *maganda*," laughs Nusrat. "You know the type. They are macho and wear gold chains around their necks."

The night has grown chilly. Habib removes his sweater and places it over my shoulders. "Orhan told me that you and Joy are wealthy Americans sent by Wendy to buy land in Kalkan."

"If we're so wealthy," quips Joy, "why would we run the Sun Pension?"

"So no one will think you're rich, and you'll get a better deal for the land, of course." Habib's tone becomes serious. "Watch out for Orhan," he says, brushing a strand of hair from my forehead.

Before I can ask why, Habib turns to Nusrat.

"*Camii-mi?*" He picks up his empty glass and raps it on the bar. "Is this a mosque?"

The days pass by, and with no word from Wendy, we fall into a routine, drinking coffee on the balcony in the morning before tidying up the pension in anticipation of the guests we hope will arrive when the tourist season peaks.

Since the town shuts off its limited supply of water at noon, I've shown Joy how to fill the small water tank on the rooftop by wedging a butter knife through the spigot at the end of the water pipe.

After lunch, we slip on bathing suits and sundresses and flag down

Ali, who runs Nusrat's ferry service to Lycia Beach, the snack bar and swimming platform Nusrat owns across the harbor.

"You will have guests, soon, *Inşallah*," says Ali, as he helps us ashore before unloading cases of Efes beer and crates of tomatoes on the dock.

We drop our bags on two lounge chairs near a grove of pine trees and dive into a turquoise sea whose currents alternate between the brine of the Mediterranean and a spring of cold fresh water rising from the sea floor. A yacht glides toward us crewed by Nusrat and his wife, Leyla, a friendly young woman whom we've met a few times at Lipsos Bar.

With porcelain skin, brilliant blue eyes, and dark hair trimmed into a bob beneath a large-brimmed straw hat, Leyla could be a descendent of the Egyptian Queen Cleopatra, who met her consort Mark Antony in these waters. Nusrat, however, looks like an aging California surfer, with faded baggy shorts, a white T-shirt, a bandana tied over his balding head, and a tiny, gray-streaked ponytail at the nape of his neck.

"Orhan can be difficult," Leyla says when we join her and Nusrat at the beach bar for a drink. "I'm not surprised you don't have guests at the pension. There are much nicer places in town. The Sun Pension used to be a hostel for backpackers, but most of them now stay in Kaş."

She leans toward us and lowers her voice. "You must have guessed that Orhan is angry at Wendy for leaving him alone this summer and sending two American women to do his job. It is hard for Turkish men to understand you independent American women. You see, the man must always think he is in charge." She plucks two Dunhill cigarettes from a silver holder and offers them to us. Although we're nonsmokers, her friendly gesture seduces us into the tribal ritual.

From his pocket, Nusrat withdraws a gold lighter, flicks it open, and strikes the flint. In turn, we steady his hand to light our cigarettes.

"Nusrat's oldest son is staying with us now," says Leyla. "And next month a singer from Istanbul will visit."

She takes a long pull from her cigarette, touches the tip of her tongue with a well-manicured fingertip, removes a stray bit of tobacco, and fixes her eyes on her husband. "The Diva is an old friend from Istanbul. She and Nusrat are very close. But after the Diva goes, you must leave that dreadful pension and stay with us."

John Coltrane's saxophone wails from the CD player toward the harbor, where the ferryman's boat sputters from the dock, cutting through pearl-white waves far beyond the reach of smoke that drifts between the olive branches.

July arrives, and with it the tourist high season. Habib sends a Swedish couple with two young children to the pension. We settle them into adjoining rooms overlooking the balcony. A Turkish couple, owners of a gulet, takes another room on the second floor until their new guests arrive from Istanbul.

"I was happy to learn that the pension is still here," says the woman. "Our crews have been staying here since the seventies because the room prices are always the cheapest in town."

The added responsibility gives structure to our day and we fall into a new routine, waking at daybreak to brew pots of fresh coffee and slice fragrant melon. We make feta cheese omelets for the adults and pancakes for the children. The Turkish couple leaves after four days, but to our surprise, the Swedish family extends their stay, adding to the meager stash of revenue for Wendy.

One morning after breakfast, we take Bekir up on his offer to join him on a hike into the mountains behind Kalkan.

He waits in front of his antique shop between two eight-foot-high, hand-etched metal urns made by his brother-in-law in Gaziantep. Glossy-black, close-cropped hair recedes from his forehead, accentuating eyes the color of mahogany framed by dark lashes. He carries an air of seductive sensuality in the way he turns his wrist to show off the engraved silver cuff he wears. For a moment, he moves his hands and body in a slow belly dance to the sweet sound of a woman singing in a minor key from an apartment across the road.

Up we go through the quiet streets, past a group of men leaving the courtyard of the mosque and a gray striped cat that scurries into an alley to pick at a chicken bone. Sunbeams split the horizon. Kalkan Harbor spreads before us. Framed by steep sienna cliffs, the sea has become as opaque as an ancient metal mirror.

On a ridge leading into the mountains toward the town of Elmalı, we pass a tree tied with rags and wisps of cloth holding prayers and wishes. The sacred tree marks the way to a tomb outside the village of Elmalı that holds the bones of a dervish named Abdal Musa.

A few weeks before, Joy and I had taken the local bus through lush countryside filled with apple orchards to Musa's resting place in a grove of pines. An old man in a blue knit cap, with one of the most peaceful faces we have seen, stood at the entrance to the tomb. He pressed his hand to his heart and said, "I am a dervish, too."

We weren't sure whether he could see the stress of the past few weeks on our faces, but he had encouraged us to sit and rest with glasses of tea.

Enveloped in the scent of pine, we watched pilgrims pray before Musa's tomb, which was draped in a green cloth, the color of Islam. For the first time in weeks, we felt safe and protected, as if Musa's spirit wished for all to be well.

Savoring the astringent brew, I told Joy about my love for the poetry of the Sufi mystic Jelaluddin Rumi, who founded the order of the Whirling Dervishes; how once, when I was staying with Sami, I had taken a ten-hour bus ride from Istanbul to Konya, where Rumi taught, just so I could see the dervishes whirl.

Now I share my story with Bekir, adding that when I arrived in Konya, I learned that the dervishes performed in public only in December, during the anniversary of Rumi's death.

His face lights up. "You and Joy must come back for the festival!" he exclaims, as if Konya is a short car ride from San Diego and New Jersey. "I have a good friend from my years in the army. He lives in Konya and can get tickets. We will go together."

"I'm in," I say.

"The offer is tempting," says Joy, looking at me. "I'll make a few queries and see if I can get a writing assignment. Plus, we could do our Christmas shopping in the Grand Bazaar."

I picture Joy sitting at the dinner table with her husband and daughter, assuring them that, in addition to covering the festival, she'll return home with spices, silver jewelry, fancy pepper grinders, and carpets.

How could they say no?

Chapter Two

LYCIAN NIGHTS

A good companion shortens the longest road.

—Turkish proverb

Angie

In late July, Bekir invites us to a party at his house, in the center of town near his shop. It is a nineteenth-century Greek sea captain's home, which the locals fondly call The Ruins.

Joy and I cross the courtyard, its path of broken stones edged in damask rose bushes and swaths of dill gone to seed, and join a group of people seated on *kilim*-covered cushions and stools. In spite of our modern clothes and hairstyles, the mix of nationalities—German, Turkish, English, French—arguing, talking, and laughing in four languages recalls the grandeur of the coast in the nineteenth century, when families and their guests dined late into the summer nights.

Bekir introduces another of Wendy's American friends, Kate, who is acting as DJ and has just put on a CD of tango music. A syncopated beat and the sound of an accordion are met by the romantic voice of Ibrahim Özgür singing "Mavi Kelebek," "Blue Butterfly." As couples get up to dance, Kate explains that she came by minibus from Kaş, twenty miles east.

"Wendy tried to convince me to rent a room at the Sun Pension for the summer," Kate says with a wry smile. "But I've been staying in the same hotel in Kaş for five years, so I turned down the invitation. From the way Bekir described the pension, I'm glad I did."

She gives each of us her card, and, turning back to the music, adds, "When you get home to the States, you're always welcome to stay with me if you're ever in San Francisco."

While Joy and Bekir settle into a game of backgammon, Habib waves from the porch and motions for me to sit next to him.

Doğan, who had been giving Joy advice on backgammon strategy, strides over. He looks like an Ottoman pirate, with his red-and-white-striped shirt tucked into tight jeans and a bandana tied over wavy, blond hair.

"Ahngee, what are you doing with this guy?" he teases, and slides a chair close to Habib and me.

When Habib casually drapes an arm over my shoulder, Doğan jumps to his feet. "You are letting him touch you. Do not play games. You must choose one of us."

Doğan's exaggerated response doesn't surprise me. As a single woman, I'm aware that there's an added question: Who might win my affection?

I've become fond of Habib and meet him for a drink almost every evening at Lipsos or at his hotel's rooftop bar, but I've grown cautious since ending my relationship with Sami. Now Doğan has forced my hand. While the waxing moon rises above the limestone cliffs, I lean my head against Habib's shoulder and choose him, if not for a lifetime, at least for the summer.

Relieved that he no longer needs to woo me, Doğan wanders back to the backgammon table. Later, I hear him offer to walk Kate to the bus station for her ride back to Kaş.

"If the bus has already left, I will be honored to drive you home," I hear him say.

A few days later, we return from Lycia Beach to find a fax from Wendy tucked under the ashtray on the front desk, apparently by Orhan. "I'm in Greece," Wendy explains. "And my clients will dock this afternoon in the harbor on the *İpek* gulet. Would you please greet them and send them to Orhan's restaurant?"

It's the least we can do for Wendy, so we dress and head down to the harbor. On the wide stern of the *İpek*, we find three deeply tanned couples from Southern California lounging on plush yellow and turquoise cushions. A woman with wavy, chin-length silver hair and dressed in an embroidered caftan gets up to pour us glasses of wine, happy to meet other Americans with whom she can share her stories.

"We just finished a marvelous five-day cruise," she says, settling back into her cushion next to her husband, who is wearing pressed khakis and a crisp white polo shirt with the collar turned up.

"Can you believe we saw Santa Claus's Mediterranean getaway?" she adds. "It's the highlight of my trip. Wait until I tell the grandkids."

They had docked at Demre, home of a fourth-century bishop, Nicholas, who cared for the poor and became known as St. Nick, the patron saint of children. Later, German immigrants brought St. Nick to America, where he gained a belly and a red suit and was transformed into Santa Claus.

During the conversation, the group asks for restaurant recommendations. We had stopped by Orhan's restaurant the night before and found his maître d' hunched over a table next to a display case containing trays of listless eggplant and tomato dishes pooled in oil. In the fish case, a sad-looking mullet stared through the glass with dull, vacant eyes. Still, we dutifully suggest they have dinner at the restaurant.

"You can't miss it," I say. "Look for the turquoise tablecloths."

One of the husbands asks about carpet shopping and bargaining. "Figure out how much you want to spend before you walk into a shop," says Joy, "and if you like to bargain, have fun. I love every carpet I've bought, and when I get home, I always wish I'd bought more."

Before we leave, I give them the name of a shop where we've bought carpets and are friendly with the owner.

In the morning we run into Orhan at the market. His half smile catches us off guard. Muscular and lean, he has a romantic face with moody brown eyes and chiseled features, softened by a dimple in his chin.

"Did the Americans eat at your restaurant last night?" we ask.

"No." His voice chills the air. "They bought carpets. But you already know this. How much money did you make?"

"What do you mean?" asks Joy, taken aback.

"I told Wendy about you," he says, and stalks away.

The night before, when we left the *İpek*, we had waved hello to Orhan's maître d' and told him about Wendy's clients. They must have skipped the restaurant and gone directly to the carpet shop.

Tour guides typically send clients to carpet dealers with whom they've made an arrangement for commissions, and we're aware that merchants fiercely guard their territory. Years ago, when I was in Cappadocia, a squabble between tour operators over clients resulted in one stabbing the other to death.

Later, at Lycia Beach, Habib confirms our suspicions and shares that Orhan stopped by his hotel. "Orhan says you're taking his carpet sale commissions so you can buy land in Kalkan. I told him that was ridiculous, but what if you were? Doesn't everyone have a right to earn their own money?"

"It's not true," I say.

"I know," he says, with a mischievous grin. "You can live here for years, but you are not considered an official local until someone spreads gossip about you. Congratulations. Tonight at Lipsos, you'll be the stars of deer chat."

The rumor that we're looking for property works in our favor. People become friendlier, telling us about uncles who have land with the most beautiful views and how they will make us a very good offer.

After too many long, hot days serving tourists, late nights drinking rakı, and endless gossip, the residents of Kalkan have become restless. They need high drama to carry them to the end of the season and are rewarded when the Diva arrives, settling into the guest room of Nusrat and Leyla's villa.

A passionate interpreter of Anatolian *arabesk*—songs of love and loss—the Diva soon wears her welcome thin with Leyla when she flirts shamelessly with Nusrat, who relishes his reputation as Kalkan's playboy and has done nothing to calm Leyla's anxiety. Angrily, Leyla insists the Diva find new lodgings.

Sensing a sympathetic ear and quick to seek a new male ally, the Diva monopolizes Habib's time.

"It is terrible the way Nusrat flirts with me in front of his wife," says the Diva. "But the little sparrow is too thin. She must put on some weight so his eyes don't wander."

"She's using all of you," I say when Habib announces that the Diva has moved in with his friend Ayşe, a woman who manages a hotel in the center of town and is always a little too eager to help him.

"When you hear her sing, you will understand why we will do anything for her," says Habib. "She will sing at Lipsos tonight. Her songs will break your heart. And," he adds, sounding like a used car salesman, "she also sings Broadway show tunes."

Nusrat sits on a barstool, having switched from his usual bartender's uniform of black pants and black T-shirt to a white linen shirt and beige linen pants. Women arrive in tight, slinky dresses. Bekir, too, has prepared for the Diva's arrival. In a blue silk shirt and black trousers, he carries a drum under his arm.

A horn honks. Like Moses parting the Red Sea, the Diva's black Mercedes parts the crowd and proceeds slowly through it. The car stops. A strappy black stiletto pump emerges, encasing a petite foot and thick ankle. The Diva steps from the car in tight black capri pants and a one-size-too-small, bubble-gum-colored scoop-neck top. Well-padded breasts push up and out, threatening to topple her forward.

Tonight she is a fairytale genie, sister to the jinn who inhabit the Anatolian countryside placing spells on mortals. Blinking gray, kohl-rimmed eyes framed by heavy, dark eyelashes, she scans the crowd and smiles at Habib, who immediately smiles back.

The men ignore her thickening middle and the extra flesh of her upper arms. They swoon when she swishes her black ponytail tied with a pink velvet ribbon.

Nusrat, with an acoustic guitar now slung over his shoulder and without Leyla, rushes over and leads the Diva to a stool behind the bar.

"*Teşekkür ederim*—thank you." The Diva closes her eyes, parts her lips, and pauses. A husky note rises from her throat and hangs in the hot, humid air.

Nusrat's guitar releases chords that flow in counterpoint to her voice. Her breasts heave. "*İçin, için yanıyor*," she sings. "*Yanıyor bu gönlüm.*"

Bekir picks up the beat on his drum and translates: "My insides burn with love for you. My heart burns with love."

The Diva's voice rises like wind blowing across the Anatolian plain in winter, opening passages deep within our veins.

She ends her performance with a surprise tribute. "Is up to you, New, York, Neeew-Yoooork," she sings, opening her arms and grinning at Joy and me.

Habib jumps to his feet. "Bravo," he calls, and the crowd joins in.

The Diva downs a rakı, slaps the glass on the bar, and hugs Nusrat. "Thank you for allowing me to sing," she says, and slinks toward Habib.

"I'm so glad you enjoyed my performance." She reaches up to kiss him on each cheek, giving a third kiss usually reserved for intimate friends.

"It was one of your best, canım," says Habib.

I bring him a fresh drink and twine my arm around his waist. The Diva forces a condescending smile at me before the chauffeur escorts her to the Mercedes, where she settles into the passenger seat.

A waiter hurries from the kitchen carrying a bucket of water to be poured in front of the car, a gesture that says, "May your path flow smoothly."

The car pulls away.

The Diva waves a well-manicured hand through the open sunroof.

"*Bekle*, wait!" yells the waiter, heaving the bucket a little too late and a little too high.

Water cascades over the car through the sunroof, spilling over the Diva's head, flattening her ponytail. Mascara streaks her face.

Joy catches my eye, then Habib's.

"Perhaps we've started a new tradition," he says, and gallantly walks toward the Mercedes.

"Angie!"

Joy's panicked voice wakes me from a disturbing dream in which someone is pounding on my bedroom door.

Sticky with sweat, I get up and open the door to find her standing outside my room.

"A man tried to get in. He kept banging on my door and asked to come in until I demanded he stop. Then I heard a door slam shut. Shh," she says, cautiously leading me to the room across the hall.

We press our ears against the door and hear deep, congested snoring.

In the morning, as we're making coffee, a man we recognize as a friend of Orhan's emerges from the room in a stained T-shirt, reeking of cigarettes and rakı. With a slight smile, he runs his fingers through sleep-tousled hair, reaches past me, and grabs a cup. Ignoring us, he pours coffee from the half-filled carafe and walks out of the pension.

"I think it's time we leave," Joy says after a long silence. "I'll send Wendy an e-mail and explain what happened."

Later, at Lycia Beach, we ask Leyla if we can take her up on the offer of a room. "I am so very sorry," she says. "But Nusrat has agreed to host another singer, this one an up-and-coming rock and roller from Izmir."

Bekir offers Joy a room at The Ruins, while Habib suggests I stay with him in his hotel. "You must leave this place immediately," he says over the phone when I tell him about the unwanted guest.

Uneasily, Joy and I return to the pension and pack our belongings, leaving behind the recipes for muffins and frittatas and the last of the Peet's Coffee. We count the money we've collected, give it to Habib for safekeeping, and send an e-mail to Wendy.

Although Habib and I have grown close, he's given no indication that our relationship is anything more than a summer romance. Often, when we're together, his friend Ayşe calls to ask for advice about her children and "terrible" ex-husband. But Habib's and my living-in-the-moment relationship unexpectedly deepens. On one of our last nights together, we hold each other in bed. He kisses my forehead, and I finally bring up Sami, explaining my reluctance to become involved again in a cross-cultural relationship.

Angrily, Habib lets go of me and reaches for a half-empty pack of

Marlboros on the nightstand. "Why have you not told me about this man before?" he asks. Like a petulant teenager, he removes a cigarette, puts it between his lips, and lights it.

Could his first hint of jealousy be aimed at me for not telling him about my past, or is it damaged pride from knowing that he isn't the first Turkish man I've been with? I know that both of us are anticipating the loss we'll feel when I leave. So I dismiss the rebuff and slide an arm teasingly over his shoulder. He stubs out his cigarette and kisses me.

During our last days in Kalkan, Joy helps Bekir in his shop while Habib and I spend nearly all of our time together. Habib introduces his niece, Ebru, an architect, and her husband, Levent, a diver for the Turkish navy. They are on holiday from Istanbul. Ebru endears herself with her quick wit and humor, so similar to Habib's, and soon I'm invited to stay with her and Levent anytime I travel through Istanbul.

"I think you understand my uncle's nature," Ebru says when we gather at Habib's rooftop bar for my good-bye celebration. "He takes care of everybody, but really he needs someone to care for him. And you make him laugh."

While Joy buys roasted hazelnuts for the bus ride from the nut seller's cart in front of the post office, I call Habib.

"Stay, at least until the weekend," he says. "Ebru and Levent can take the bus back to Istanbul with you. Anyway, you promised to come to my hotel and say good-bye."

"But the bus leaves in twenty minutes," I say.

The tone in his voice makes it clear: He knows as well as I do that if I see him, I'll change my mind and stay. And what good would it do?

With mixed feelings, I reluctantly decline.

Outside his shop, Bekir embraces us. "Do not worry, my friends," he says, when we reluctantly let go. "I will see you in December for the dervish festival. I've contacted my friend in Konya. He will get our tickets."

When Joy and I reach the bus station, we find Leyla waiting in tight jeans and a halter top beneath a blue neon sign for our bus, Kâmil Koc, featuring a yellow camel, its legs in full stride.

"I wish you a safe and blessed journey, my friends," she says, and holds up a small crystal bottle of water.

She unscrews the cap and pours the liquid in front of our feet. "*Güle, güle*. Go smiling, smiling. But please come back one day."

Then she hops into her Jeep and roars off toward Lycia Beach, a dark-eyed young man, the singer from Izmir, by her side.

A week after I return to San Diego, a message blinks on my answering machine. Habib's all-too-familiar voice says he's heard from Bekir that I'm coming back to Turkey in December.

"Is it true?" he asks.

Joy calls to say that Bekir sent her an e-mail. His friend Mahmut has indeed bought tickets for the dervish festival, and she's managed to get a writing assignment to cover it. Bekir has also invited us to visit his family in Gaziantep.

"He told me his sister will teach us how to make *icli kofte*, with fresh minced lamb," says Joy, mirth filling her voice. "He said that she is one of the best cooks in all of Turkey."

And while Wendy has yet to return our messages, Joy and I talk on the phone several times a week, catching up on the latest news from our Turkish friends and making plans for our December trip.

Chapter Three

BEFORE AND AFTER

This horror will grow mild, this darkness light.
—*John Milton*, Paradise Lost

Joy
September 11, 2001

On a Mediterranean-blue-sky morning in central New Jersey, I'm at my desk on a writing deadline. The windows are open and the scent of sweet autumn clematis drifts into the room. Instead of staring at my computer screen, I'm thinking about how, if I squint at the sky in just the right way, I can pretend I'm back on the Lycian coast.

My daughter, Sarah, is at school, and my husband, Fred, is at his office just outside New York City. The birds sing and the cat curls up on the chair. I surf the web for a while, answer a few e-mails, and finally focus on my work.

A few minutes past nine, the phone rings. Angie's name appears on the caller ID. It's just after six a.m. in California. She's up early, I think as I pick up the receiver.

"Can you believe this is happening?" she asks, her voice strained.

"What are you talking about?" I say, imagining every conceivable natural disaster in California. "Has there been an earthquake?"

"No. My sister just called from Oregon. A plane has crashed into the World Trade Center. They think it's a terrorist attack. Another plane is heading toward San Francisco!"

"Slow down," I say, taking in the gravity of her words.

Phone in hand, I turn on the television and see smoke billowing through the familiar streets of lower Manhattan.

I tell Angie I'll call back and immediately phone my mother, who's just heard the news. I call Fred, who has colleagues in the first tower. He says he can see smoke from his office. I call Sarah's high school. The secretary says the kids are safe and will be sent home at noon. I think of our friends who work in the city, friends who work in the towers, friends with children.

Feeling simultaneously empty and panicked, I take a breath. Later, I stand in front of the television and watch the towers fall again and again—images so unbelievable, they seem new each time the cycle repeats itself.

My cell phone rings. I answer.

"Canım, my dear, are you all right? How is your family? *Allah Allah.*"

"Bekir?" I say. My breath catches in my throat. My eyes sting.

"We are seeing what happened. It is all over the news," he says. "We are so worried about you and Angie. Doğan is here, too. Who would do such a terrible thing? We are sending our love and prayers."

After I hang up, I sit down and write a note in my journal: The first two people to call me are Angie and Bekir.

Because I've given talks on religion, including Islam and Sufism, in the days that follow I'm invited to many interfaith group meetings and speak with members of the Muslim community who have lost loved ones in the towers. "This was an act of terror by crazy people," we all agree.

"Are you and Angie still going to Turkey in December?" friends ask.

"We already have our tickets," I say, but I hesitate. I have a husband and daughter to think about.

"I've spoken to Bekir and Ebru," Angie says when I phone and mention my concerns. "They said everyone is so sad this happened, and they promise to take good care of us."

She reminds me that after the first Gulf War broke out, she had gone to Kenya and Tanzania in East Africa.

"In spite of the travel warnings, I'm glad I went," she says, adding that with few tourists, she had had the game parks almost to herself. "I really got to know the people and never had to worry for a moment about my safety."

As September becomes October and November and the airlines institute new security policies, Angie and I formulate our itinerary. We have long discussions about our own fears, but they have more to do with flying in a plane than traveling in Turkey.

My husband is skeptical, but Sarah comes home from school one day and says, "I told my social studies teacher you were going to Turkey next month. She asked if I was scared, and I said maybe a little, but that you have lots of friends there. And besides, you'll be with Angie and Bekir."

The trust in her eyes and words gives me the go-ahead I need.

December
2001

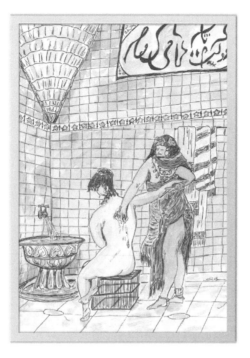

Chapter Four

THE STEAMY SIDE OF ISTANBUL

*There were many amongst them as exactly proportion'd as ever
any Goddess was drawn by the pencil of Guido or Titian,
and most of their skins shiningly white, only adorn'd by their Beautiful Hair divided into many tresses hanging on their
shoulders, braided either with pearl or riband, perfectly
representing the figures of the Graces.*

—*Lady Mary Wortley Montagu,* "The Ladys Coffeehouse";
or, the Turkish Baths, The Turkish Embassy Letters

Joy

Three weeks before Christmas, Angie and I wait in a long security line at John F. Kennedy International Airport. There is yet to be a shoe bomber or a liquid bomber, so we're not required to unlace and remove our shoes or discard our full-size face creams. But there are new security measures: a careful, slow flip through our passports; intense scrutiny of our passport photos and us; X-rayed backpacks; a handbag search; and a body check with a magnetic baton that discovers a set of car keys in my winter coat.

On the other side of security, fellow passengers survey one another with relief and perhaps the smallest hint of suspicion. "I'm not a terrorist," our eyes seem to say. "Are you?"

By the time Angie and I settle into our seats, we've escaped a final insult to our sanity: an unending loop of a single song, Burl Ives singing "Have a Holly Jolly Christmas," streaming from speakers hidden between rows of cosmetics counters and shelves of tax-free liquor in the duty-free shop. But we can't escape the couple in front of us on the plane, who tilt their seats back as far as they will go, making it impossible to stretch our legs, and launching us into plans to soothe our cramped muscles in the warmth of a Turkish bath as soon as we arrive in Istanbul.

Angie picks up a conversation about Habib we'd begun the day before. "I called him to let him know we're coming to Istanbul," she sighs, "but he never called back. His niece Ebru sent an e-mail, though. She and Levent invited us for dinner before we leave for the dervish festival. She'll bring me up to date on Habib, although I may not want the news."

I'm hoping, too, to get word about Wendy. Her e-mail address is no longer working, and Bekir has shared that she and Orhan closed the Sun Pension just after September 11.

The whirr of the plane's engines lulls us toward sleep. I shift my legs, thinking of Fred and Sarah at home in their beds under down quilts. The woman next to me slumps in her seat, leaning her head toward my shoulder. I move closer to Angie, who's nodding off.

Hamam, the Turkish word for bath, means spreader of warmth. I drift into a dream of white marble walls, steam caressing my skin and opening pores, masseuses smoothing away all the aches the airline industry has inflicted on my body.

Our taxi enters Sultanahmet, Istanbul's oldest quarter, through Cat-ladi Kapi, the cracked-marble gate. It rumbles over cobbled streets once traversed by emperors, sultans, and courtesans and stops in front of our hotel, just inside the red-stone Byzantine seawall.

Enveloped in translucent light and the scent of sea and spices, we're tempted to stretch out on the thick gold and green bedspreads and watch snowflakes drift past the minarets of the Blue Mosque, just beyond our hotel room window. Before jetlag pulls us into honey-thick sleep, we leave the hotel and walk through Gülhane Park toward the Çemberlitaş Hamam.

A sharp wind has picked up, bringing dampness from the Bosporus. Clouds spit snowflakes into the air. A group of university students waits for the tram in a montage of black and gray coats and dark headscarves, looking as if they're posing for a portrait by one of Istanbul's great twentieth-century photographers, Ara Güler.

When we reach the corner where the Çemberlitaş bath should be, we lose our bearing even though we've seen its namesake from blocks away: the imposing Çemberlitaş tower, erected by the first emperor of Byzantium, Constantine the Great, to mark the *Divanyolu*, the "Imperial Road" that led to Rome.

Noticing our confusion, a chestnut vendor points us down a dank flight of steps behind a row of storefronts. At the bottom we enter a dimly lit lobby, where an elderly man with a trimmed gray beard and a crocheted cap pulled tight to his skull takes our money. We buy the works: steam bath, massage, and shampoo.

The man hands us massage tokens and directs us past a group of German tourists arguing vigorously about whether they should pay the extra money for a massage or not. An apple-cheeked girl wearing round, wire-rimmed glasses and a flowered headscarf waits in the doorway of the women's lounge.

"Lütfen, please," she says sweetly, "follow this way," and she leads us into a narrow, musty room more reminiscent of our high school gym locker rooms than of Ottoman luxury.

Gone are the lattice-screened changing rooms of my imagination, with their soft cushions on chaise longues and cups of hot, sweet tea. Instead, the girl offers scratchy, red-plaid towels called *peştemals* and motions us to choose from a stock of cheap, plastic flip-flops lined up beneath the lockers.

"Lütfen," she says, turning to two Italian women drying their hair. "Lockers are for these ladies now."

One of the women glances up, letting us know she has no intention of rushing.

"Take your time," I say, but in truth I'm cold and tired and wish she'd hurry.

Five German women enter and jostle for space, which seems to encourage the Italian woman to finish drying thick, golden-chestnut-colored strands. I run my hand through my own fine, lank hair as she shimmies her slim body into a skintight leather skirt and soft cashmere sweater. A final flip of her hair and she slinks past the German women, who rush toward the lockers that now belong to Angie and me.

A competitive gene switches on. With a head start on the German women, we quickly remove tights, skirts, sweaters, and underwear before attempting to cover our goose-fleshed bodies with the stiff, postage-sized peştemals. Designed to protect a woman's modesty on the short walk from the changing room to the bath, these peştemals are so small, they barely cover our derrieres.

"I feel like a stuffed grape leaf," says Angie, attempting as best she can to secure the towel ends under her armpits.

"Me, too," I say, slipping on a pair of damp rubber slippers. I tie my hair into a ponytail and pad behind Angie through a cold, clammy antechamber. When Angie heaves open the heavy wooden door of the steam room, hot, moist air catches in my throat. White marble walls and a high domed ceiling echo and amplify a rhythmic chant of dripping water and the beehive hum of foreign voices.

Like apparitions, women lie head to toe on the large, hexagon-shaped platform of gray-veined marble called the belly stone. Breasts angle in all directions. Pubic hair frizzes and fluffs in the humid air.

We cross the threshold through a cloud of steam to a vacant alcove, one of a half-dozen containing marble basins and faucets. Time changes shape, stretches and bends. We could be in the sixteenth century, at the height of the Ottoman Empire, when the sultan's architect, Mimar Sinan, a contemporary of Michelangelo and Leonardo da Vinci, designed the Çemberlitaş Hamam. The baths were an essential part of spiritual ritual for Muslim men and women who purified their bodies before Friday prayers. But the baths held special importance for women. Except for a weekly trip to the hamam, women were sequestered in their homes, away from contact with unrelated men or infidels. Men were forbidden to enter the women's baths and faced execution if they did.

In the safety of the hamam, women gauged the pulse of the neighborhood and learned the latest medical cures. A mother of an eligible son would examine a prospective daughter-in-law and potential bearer of her grandchildren in the most intimate detail by dropping a bar of soap and observing the shape of the girl's breasts and hips as she picked it up.

Women brought carpets, towels, henna for hair and hands, attar of rose to perfume their bodies, as well as sophisticated lunches of roast chicken, pilaf, and sweetmeats. A beautiful, green-eyed Circassian girl from the Caucasus, north of the Black Sea, or a jet-black Nubian woman from the banks of the Nile, would lead their wealthy clients to a changing room with polished lattice screens, sculpted fountains, and ornate wooden chaise longues piled with embroidered pillows.

While the lady drank tea from a delicate glass cup, her servant helped remove clothes and shoes, wrapping her in a robe of spun silk, and slipped wooden platform sandals inlaid with silver and mother of pearl over her feet to protect her delicate soles from the hot floor of the steam room. When her patron was fully relaxed, the servant would guide her through a dark passage to the great marble bath, with its domed ceiling and waves of gauzy light.

Our towels are already damp by the time we sit down at a basin below the domed alcove and turn on the elaborate brass faucets. Above, star-shaped vents unleash hot air into the sky. A light bulb sways from the center of the dome on a long electrical cord. As I fill the basin with a mixture of hot and cold water, I remember something Bekir told me.

"Until I was seven," he said, "I came to the women's hamam with my mother. While my friends and I played, we also watched the women, their bodies and how they moved, how they shampooed their hair, and the water falling across the marble. We listened to the gossip, too. At wedding times, the women painted their hands and feet with henna and teased the bride-to-be about her wedding night." He smiled. "It is how I learned to love the body and the heart of a woman."

Angie adjusts the taps and fills a red plastic bowl with a round indentation molded in the center for gripping. The elegant *hamam tasları*—bowls hammered by Armenian craftsmen from copper, silver, or tin—are now collector's items. In the twenty-first-century hamam, they've been replaced with garish but functional plastic replicas. Angie hands me another bowl. We pour the water through our hair and over our faces, letting it fall over backs and breasts, sliding over skin toward drains built into the marble floor.

From the raised marble belly stone, a woman sits up and wags an index finger. At first we ignore her and dip the bowl back into the basin. She shakes her head back and forth, while patting her hand on the stone. Her silent mime reminds us that according to hamam protocol, the rinse at the basin comes after the steam bath and massage, not before.

Reluctant to give up the sensuous pleasure of cool water on hot skin, we climb onto the belly stone and carefully pick our way toward the center. Smiling, the woman moves closer to her teenage daughter and makes room on the crowded platform, where we spread out our peştemals and lie down, pressing our backs against warm marble. Her face flushed crimson, the woman whispers something to her daughter, who laughs at their private joke and reaches for her mother's hand.

Delicate stretch marks adorn the mother's breasts like tribal scars; her navel creases like a smile into a soft mound of flesh as her belly rises up and down. Her daughter, with budding breasts and scant pubic hair, rearranges a fawn-colored ponytail. Taut muscles move beneath sleek skin as she turns onto her stomach and brushes a wisp of hair from her mother's forehead.

Touching the flesh of my own belly, I think of a morning long ago in a hotel in Athens, when my then eight-year-old daughter and I had taken a bath, lathering each other's hair, shaping the strands into question marks above our heads. She had burst into laughter when the soapy question mark toppled over my forehead, had smoothed it from my face in a gesture as motherly as any I had shared with her.

The air has grown heavy, filling our lungs with moisture. We notice the scent of perfume, unguents, soap, and something richer rising from pores of the women surrounding us, the primal scent of saltwater, brine, and algae. Then we detect the acrid smell of tobacco rising from skin. Our world of deodorants, powders, and body sprays hasn't prepared us for this assault to our senses.

The door to the steam room slams open and four German women burst through it, joking and climbing onto the stone. Elbows, knees, and peştemals scatter in all directions. Two women with short, spiky blonde haircuts squeeze behind us in the winding row leading to the masseuses.

We're fascinated by the ease and confidence these women have in their bodies. At home, to be naked means to engage in a competition to become the thinnest, to crave cellulite-free thighs and large, perfect breasts, to dwell in a sense of inadequacy that only leads to shame and self-judgment. But here, pleasure seems to matter more than shame. A wrinkle here, cellulite there, a mole on your hip bone—it all looks elegant in an envelope of steam.

By the time we near the edge of the platform, our skin drips with sweat, soaking our towels. The mother and daughter move in one direction while we wait behind a petite Japanese woman who slides to the edge of the belly stone for her turn with a skinny masseuse wearing a matching red bra and panties. The masseuse fills a pillowcase with soap and water and squeezes mounds of suds over the woman until she disappears beneath the lather. With a coarse mitt, the masseuse gently polishes the woman's skin, carefully kneading thighs and buttocks and back.

Angie nods in the direction of another masseuse on the opposite side of the stone who commands the teenage girl to lie down. The masseuse bends forward. Rolls of fat fold over her belly button, eclipsing her black bikini underwear. Heavy breasts swing back and forth as she roughly massages the girl's back with a nubby cotton mitt like she's kneading a mound of bread dough. She slaps the girl's bottom, indicating that she should turn onto her back, and continues to scrub belly, breasts, and arms until the girl's skin takes on the color of a beet.

"I'm glad we're on this side of the platform," I whisper, glancing toward the gentle, skinny masseuse.

We've been in hamams in Istanbul and on the Mediterranean coast, but we've never seen a hamam so crowded. We're next in line and wait while the gentle, skinny masseuse leads the Japanese woman to a basin for shampoo and rinsing. When the masseuse finishes, she motions for Angie and me to take our places on the edge of the stone. Before I have a chance to move, one of the German women sits up. Her plump breasts fall forward.

"Please. We are in a hurry," she says anxiously. "Our boyfriends are waiting for us. And we are already late."

"May we go ahead?" asks her friend.

Without waiting for a reply, they clamber over us. Their pink faces shine with sweat, and they look like they might expire at any moment from heat exhaustion.

The skinny masseuse takes the women's massage tokens and drops them into her cup.

But the large masseuse has been keeping a close watch and has already pegged the German women as her clients. When she sees that her co-worker has claimed her clients, she walks over, hands on hips, breasts swaying, belly fat jiggling. She grabs one of the German women by the right arm and pulls her toward the opposite side of the platform.

Shaking her cup full of tokens, the skinny masseuse grabs the woman's left arm and tugs back. At the end of the night, those tokens will be redeemed for cash, and the skinny masseuse is not about to lose them.

Conversation on the platform stops. The masseuses shout back and forth, their voices echoing against marble. With no resolution in sight, someone has called the locker room attendant, who emerges from the mist, her glasses opaque with steam.

"Ladies," she says, looking at us and pointing to the large masseuse, "you must go with her."

Her breath ragged from excitement, the large masseuse turns, looks at us, and scowls. A serious debate begins until tokens are exchanged and she and her adversary reach a compromise. The German women return to the skinny masseuse. Expecting the worst, we inch off the belly stone and follow the large masseuse to the opposite side of the platform.

I slide to the edge of the stone and lie on my back while the masseuse fills her muslin pillowcase with soapy water and squeezes, immersing me in suds. My nose tickles and I sneeze.

"Where you from?" she asks in a gruff voice, digging hard knuckles into my thighs and pressing my hip bones against the marble.

"America, near New York City," I say. I suddenly feel lightheaded.

The masseuse remains silent. I wince at the pressure of her hands on my thighs. Soap bubbles tickle my nose, and I wonder what she's thinking. Perhaps that the attacks on the World Trade Center were justified? Or, am I just another body that will allow her to pay bills at the cost of tired, swollen feet and an aching back?

She massages my breasts and shoulders and taps my hip, indicating that I should turn onto my stomach.

"I am so sorry about what has happened in your country," she finally says. "My brother, he lives in the New York. It is a great city like Istanbul, yes?" She points to her cup of tokens. "One day, I will go there."

Lost, perhaps, in thoughts of a family reunion in a faraway land, the masseuse softly hums, gently working my aching hips and rubbing my tired feet and toes. She leads me to a basin to wait while she takes her time with Angie, singing in rhythm to the movement of her hands.

After shampooing and rinsing our hair, she sits between us for a moment at the basin, pressing our palms to her flushed cheeks. "Maybe one day I will see you in America," she says.

"İnşallah, God willing," I smile.

Still singing, she leaves us and greets her next client, who is already waiting on the edge of the platform.

On our way toward the door, we pass the German women, who linger at one of the basins, filling their plastic bowls with soothing, lukewarm water. Forgetting boyfriends waiting outside in the cold, they close their eyes and tilt their heads back in what we can only believe to be bliss.

Chapter Five

BLINIS IN BEYOĞLU

If it didn't happen in Turkey, it didn't happen.
—*Marion Craven, docent, Mingei Gallery,
Balboa Park, California*

Angie

The morning call to prayer reverberates across rooftops from the loudspeakers of the Blue Mosque, stirring us from dreams. "La ilaha Illa 'Llah . . ."

I rise and pull open the heavy curtains. Corrugated metal rooftops gleam in the dawn light. Outside the city wall, the Sea of Marmara sparkles like melting ice. Fishing trawlers and oil freighters glide across the sea toward the Bosporus, the narrow strait that splits the city of Istanbul between two continents—Europe and Asia.

Joy orders coffee, rolls, *beyaz peynir* (sheep's milk cheese), and olives from room service. When breakfast arrives, we sip our coffee and I unfold a map of Turkey. While I mark our route toward Konya, Joy immerses herself in Rumi's poetry, reading aloud:

O soul, from where has come to you this new breath?

O heart, from where has come this heavy throbbing?

O bird, speak now the language of the birds . . .

The phone rings, jolting us from thirteenth-century Konya to the present. I pick up the receiver and hear the cheerful voice of Habib's niece Ebru. "Levent and I made reservations for dinner tonight," she says. "Our treat, so you can't say no."

Ebru has also arranged for her friend Simla, a former English professor and tour guide, to take us shopping this afternoon in the Grand Bazaar.

"And when you're through," adds Ebru, "Levent and I will meet you for dinner at Rejans, near my office, on the European side of the Bosporus. You'll love Rejans."

She explains that the restaurant was founded by three Russian dancers who escaped to France during the Bolshevik Revolution before settling in Istanbul. "They serve blinis and caviar with a Turkish flare."

"And the best lemon vodka south of the Caucasus," Levent chimes in from an extension.

"Did she say anything about Habib?" Joy asks after I hang up.

I shake my head as if the thought hadn't occurred to me. Since Ebru hadn't mentioned him, I was too proud to ask.

Turning back to the map, I try to push Habib out of my mind, but my thoughts and yellow marker drift toward the Mediterranean coast. What if I'd extended my visa and stayed in Kalkan? What if I were a little more reckless and a little less sensible? No regrets, I tell myself, and begin to plan our route east.

When Simla meets us in the lobby of our hotel, we feel an instant kinship with her.

A petite woman in her early sixties with raven-black hair brushing the shoulders of a black herringbone suit jacket, Simla smiles easily, kisses our cheeks, and insists on ordering tea before we venture onto the rainy streets of Sultanahmet.

Lifting her teacup to matte red lips, she explains how, at thirty-two, she became a widow with two small children and was forced to leave a job she loved, as a poorly paid professor of English literature, for a more lucrative job in tourism.

Later, as she leads us through the crowded streets of the seventy-acre, covered Grand Bazaar, she muses on her life as a guide. "In many ways, I feel as though I am still teaching literature," she says. "Or perhaps I should say I gather stories. Every shop owner has one."

We pass shops selling fabric, leather coats, pottery, and glass and brass coffee grinders. Carpet sellers call Simla's name, but she dismisses them with a flick of her hand. "We're going to see Osman," she says.

Past an elegant shop selling soaps made of olive oil and laurel and thick white Turkish towels, we turn a corner and stop in front of a window where a large silk carpet shimmers in shades of sand, walnut, and ocher.

The shop appears to be closed, but Simla opens the door and calls her friend Osman's name. We step inside. A tall man rises from a desk in the corner, next to a pile of red and black patterned kilims.

"Simla, merhaba, hello," he says.

And to us, "Good afternoon."

His soft voice carries a hint of the Scottish highlands, where, he says, he studied English literature at the University of Edinburgh before returning to Istanbul.

"And that is how we met—here at the university," adds Simla.

Osman gives Simla a tender smile before sending one of his assistants to fetch tiny cups of Turkish coffee. "Like Simla, I have two daughters. My wife and I wanted our daughters to go to school abroad and experience the world," he says. "But I could not have afforded this on a professor's salary. And I always loved carpets, the beautiful patterns and how the symbols of women, animals, birds, and Allah are woven into them."

He shrugs and looks around the shop as if this explains or justifies why he turned to commerce, then leans an elbow on a stack of Anatolian kilims and crosses a loafered foot over his ankle. In wide-wale corduroys, blue check oxford shirt, and off-white cable knit sweater, his thick brown hair shot with silver, he has the professorial good looks I'm certain his female students found attractive.

When we comment on the low-key atmosphere of his shop—so unlike all the others we passed, where touts stand outside trying to snag customers off the street—he looks again at Simla, who nods her head.

"Tourists don't like to be hassled. Especially Americans," he says. "So I don't pay anyone to sit outside and bother them. I sell many carpets to American friends who work at the embassy. They trust me to send them the best that I have, at a fair price." He flips over a few carpets from the stack behind him and shows us tags with prices in Turkish liras. "These are my prices," he says with a grin. "No haggling."

After the coffee arrives, the topic moves to current political events and the fallout from September 11. Simla sets her empty demitasse on a tray and talks about how painful it was for her and Osman to see the images of burning towers and how, like Bekir and Doğan, they worried about their friends.

"The men who flew those planes are ignorant, uneducated people," says Osman.

"We have lived through difficult times, too," nods Simla. "You see, in 1980, the military staged a coup and took over our country."

Osman looks through the window and watches a boy carry empty tea glasses on a brass tray. "It was a very difficult period," he says. "But you must understand something. The coup was necessary to preserve the Turkish republic. After the Arab-Israeli war in 1973, our oil supplies were cut off. A drought had killed the wheat crop. We didn't even have bread on our tables. Of course people grew restless and started fighting in the streets. And then the shah was overthrown in Iran. We watched the Ayatollah Khomeini and his fundamentalist Islamic government rise to power. It's hard to imagine how difficult it was for all of us."

Hands animated, he continues, "People were afraid we would lose our republic. Our leaders were weak, the politicians arguing all the time. Students led protests in the streets. You see, Communism was still a romantic idea. Leftist students resented Western capitalism. And Islamic fundamentalists with support from the Middle East wanted to break down our secular government. Not even martial law could stop the killing."

Osman talks of a time when Turkey experienced 20 percent unemployment and 100 percent inflation, of peasants migrating to cities that had no infrastructures to support them, of an uneasy relationship with the West.

Interrupted by his assistant, he excuses himself and selects a few carpets for a customer from a stack near the door. Simla waits for him to return before sharing a story he has not heard before.

"I was a new teacher in those days," she says. "Students were demonstrating daily on the campuses. One morning a young man slipped into my classroom and sat down at one of the empty seats in the front row. Moments later, two armed soldiers burst in, demanding to know if I could account for all of my students."

Her voice trembles. "The boy was not from my class, but I

recognized him from campus demonstrations. He looked at me as if to say, 'Please don't let them take me away.' He might have been arrested and tortured just for demonstrating. I was so scared, but I told the soldiers, 'How dare you enter my classroom like this? You have no right and must leave at once.' The soldiers apologized and left. I almost fell apart afterwards," she adds with a slight, satisfied smile.

Osman's eyes remain fixed on Simla. "Anatolia is ancient," he says. "But our republic was only founded in 1923. With all the turmoil in the countries around us, you might say it is a miracle. We have everything here, and we must work hard to cultivate democracy. Although I want my daughters to be educated in the West like me, it is important that they bring this knowledge home to Turkey."

We leave Simla and Osman with their memories and venture into the antique wing of the Grand Bazaar, where we pause in front of a shop window filled with amber jewelry and carved meerschaum clay pipes. Inside we're surrounded by cabinets containing coral signet rings; filigreed tribal bracelets; musty, faded icons; and shelves of folios containing replicas of Ottoman miniatures painted over Ottoman-Arabic script.

"This reminds me of a print I saw in Bekir's shop," says Joy, picking up a painting of a raven-haired, winged goddess standing on the back of a bull, which, in turn, balances on a fish swimming in a lapis sea.

"Ah yes, that particular painting was made here in Istanbul," says the shop owner, Gerson Mercado, who introduces himself and offers tea.

When we tell him that Mercado doesn't sound like a Turkish surname, he smiles. "It isn't," he says. "My family is from Spain."

He excuses himself, disappears behind a heavy wool curtain into a back room, and returns with a yellowed *New York Times* newspaper clipping with the headline, "Spanish Jews Still in Istanbul 500 Years After the Inquisition."

The article explains how in 1492—the same month Christopher Columbus sailed for the West Indies and shortly after the Muslim Moors were driven out of their last stronghold, Granada, Spain—Queen Isabella and King Ferdinand issued an edict that their Spanish-Jewish subjects had three choices: convert to Catholicism, leave the country, or face execution.

Many Spanish Jews, (called *Sephardim* from the Hebrew word for Spain, *Sepharad*) decided to leave and reached out to Ottoman Sultan Beyazıt II, who invited them to resettle in Turkey. More than one hundred thousand Jews accepted his offer.

"How could you call Ferdinand of Aragon a wise king?" said the sultan. "The same Ferdinand who impoverished his own land and enriched ours?"

Under Ottoman rule, Jewish and Christian minorities thrived, adding to the wealth of the empire, and were able to practice their own religions. The Ottomans organized them into millets, separate non-Muslim communities with their own schools, religious leaders, newspapers, legal systems, and dress codes. The millet system required minorities to wear clothing that identified their religious and ethnic groups, including colored slippers. Jews wore blue slippers; Armenians, violet; Greeks, black.

What surprises us and apparently surprised the author of the *Times* article is that after a five-hundred-year family history in Turkey, Mr. Mercado still embraces his Spanish heritage.

"Before my family arrived in Istanbul, they were merchants," he says. "That is how my father chose our surname, Mercado."

Later, when we rejoin Simla in Osman's carpet shop, we talk of our meeting with Mr. Mercado. Simla suggests we visit the Zülfaris Synagogue, now converted into a museum chronicling the history of Sephardic Jews in Turkey.

Until the end of the seventeenth century, Sephardic Jews made up nearly 10 percent of Istanbul's population, most settling in Beyoğlu among Armenian, Greek, and Italian Christians. Zülfaris, meaning fringe of the bride or bridal curls in Old Turkish, was named for the Jewish brides who walked up the street to the synagogue to marry.

In contrast to the grandeur of the Hagia Sophia, Blue Mosque, and Süleymaniye Mosque, the Zülfaris Synagogue radiates intimacy and warmth. Two sparkling brass chandeliers hang from the second-floor ceiling, surrounded by small crystal hanging lamps and wall sconces.

A map of the Ottoman world shows the routes taken by the Jews across the Mediterranean and Aegean seas through the Bosporus to their place of refuge in Istanbul. An exhibit explains how David and Samuel ibn Nahmias, Sephardic Jewish brothers, founded Turkey's first printing press in 1493, causing a revolutionary change in the empire. While it made Turkey competitive with the West, the printing press hastened the demise of the calligraphy profession, one of the most esteemed professions in the Ottoman Empire.

In the upstairs gallery, used by women for worship, photographs of the congregation's past line the walls. Brides in lace dresses wear simple, beaded headpieces; stiff and formal couples pose on the synagogue steps; families picnic beneath mulberry trees along the Bosporus.

In the vestibule of the synagogue, a guest book contains impressions from visitors. A man who was refused asylum in the West during the Holocaust thanks Turkey for receiving him and saving his life. There are messages from dignitaries and religious leaders recognizing Turkey's successful efforts during the Nazi years to protect its Jewish community. And messages from travelers like us, trying to understand Turkey in light of a larger world history.

Just after sunset, we leave our hotel and hail a taxi at the Roman hippodrome. The driver speeds past Topkapı Palace, home of the Sultans, and over the Galata Bridge across the Golden Horn. The driver drops us off near the two-block-long *Tünel*, the world's shortest underground tram and the easiest route up the steep hill to Rejans, in the Beyoğlu neighborhood.

We join commuters finished with the day's work and crowd into a tramcar. In less than five minutes, we disperse into narrow streets, past apartment buildings whose facades are painted in now faded shades of aqua, green, and yellow. Wisteria vines twist through overhanging wrought iron balconies. We imagine walking these streets on a soft spring evening, perhaps with a lover, when panicles of lavender-tinted blossoms drape over the balconies like dowagers' necklaces.

Caught up in the romance of the neighborhood, we stop for a drink at the Pera Palace Hotel, where mystery writer Agatha Christie is said to have written her famous thriller *Murder on the Orient Express* in homage to the luxury train that began its journey in Paris and ended at Istanbul's Sirkeci Station. The Pera Palace had a reputation for hosting some of the world's more interesting women, including Dutch-born spy Mata Hari, who, during World War I, kept a room at the Pera and passed secrets over cocktails.

Eyes follow us when we walk into the Pera's dark, paneled bar. At a corner table, a group of businessmen drink scotch, smoke cigars, and exchange documents from leather briefcases. A woman in a fur-trimmed jacket perches on a barstool, running a fingertip around the rim of her martini glass. We settle into high-backed chairs under a tall window and order two rakı.

A British couple and their two teenage sons sit at a circular table in the center of the room and thumb through guidebooks. In heavy boots and parkas, they seem ready to hike the Yorkshire moors instead of Istanbul streets. The teenagers sip Cokes through plastic straws, feigning interest while their parents read tales of World War I espionage from a Baedeker guidebook.

A young woman in an ankle-length, black dress, and her partner, a lanky man in black trousers and a puffy-sleeved white shirt, set up instruments on the small stage. The room grows quiet with anticipation as the woman practices scales on her flute and the young man tightens the strings of his acoustic guitar.

After a few more warm-up chords, the young man settles into what sounds like a Chopin nocturne. I hum along and slip into the Pera's romantic past, imagining Russian, French, and German ambassadors, double agents, and mercenaries turning their heads toward the audacious Mata Hari.

"What is that tune?" asks Joy.

Then it gradually comes to us: "You came and you gave without taking, oh Mandy."

When the duo segues into a Paul McCartney tribute featuring the flautist trilling "When I'm Sixty-Four," the British couple sings along. Their sons slump into their seats and stare at their Cokes.

Having grown up reading Agatha Christie mysteries, we had half-convinced ourselves that we would encounter characters resembling those in *Murder on the Orient Express*, perhaps a dark-eyed chanteuse crooning Cole Porter's "Begin the Beguine." But the Pera embraces its reputation with a new rhythm.

After finishing our drinks, on our way to the lobby, we pass the woman at the bar. She has turned her attention to the adoring eyes of a man half her age, who rests his hand high on her thigh.

Ghosts linger on the streets of Beyoğlu. At the neighborhood's highest point, the Galata watchtower overlooks the Golden Horn. In the seventeenth century, a Turk, Hezârfen Ahmed Çelebi, donned wings and jumped from Galata Tower—the first successful flight over the Golden Horn.

History shifts at each corner, reminders of a time when merchants grouped together to sell a single product. On a street named Minare, "minaret," shop owners sell gleaming, gold-spiral minaret tops. On Balyoz, "hammer," burly workers move among axes, pipes, and kitchen hardware. Street names were also coined to reflect the traits of the people who ran the shops: Gönül, "willingness"; Jurnal, "informer"; Acar, "clever."

On the street of musical instruments, a Bob Dylan look-alike in a threadbare, black peacoat sits in the doorway of a music shop, plucking guitar strings. A cigarette dangles between his ring and middle finger as he searches for a chord.

To reach Rejans, we detour through the Balık Pazarı, the market, where naked light bulbs hang over crates of silvery turbot, lustrous sea bass, red mullet, and bluefish.

"*Taze balık*," a man shouts. "Fresh fish."

Joy spots Rejans tucked into in a dead-end alley in the old neighborhood of White Russian émigrés. Inside the restaurant, little seems to have changed since the 1930s. Wood paneling, high ceilings, an orchestra loft, and art nouveau wall sconces transport us back to the early twentieth century.

The maître d' seats us at a table in the center of the room. Although we're early, the attention we receive makes us think that perhaps we have stepped into an alternate universe in which we've become visiting dignitaries. A waiter, businesslike in tuxedo pants, white shirt, and a long white apron, brings the house specialty, lemon vodka, in chilled cylindrical glasses.

Moments later, the hostess, a descendant of the original owners, arrives with a plate of pale-pink fish roe salad. Her sleek, shoulder-length, graying hair is brushed away from her face, revealing high cheekbones and broad-set, pale green eyes. She speaks several languages. But English isn't one of them, and so she settles into French, the language of Ottoman diplomacy.

"*C'etait le table d'Atatürk*," she says, pointing a manicured hand toward a round table in the corner to the left of the entrance.

We picture a robust Kemal Atatürk, founder and first president of the Turkish republic, with brooding eyes and thinning hair slicked back from his wide brow. He leans over his plate of duck a l'orange with the same intensity he might have invested when negotiating the Treaty of Lausanne, which created the Republic of Turkey. From here, without being seen, Atatürk had full view of the room, which would be important if you had just overthrown a government.

The hostess's eyes grow dreamy as she describes Atatürk. "Such a gentleman," she says, as Joy translates into English. "So polite, and he loved the ladies."

Like many Turkish women of a certain age, the hostess harbors a crush on this legendary and long-deceased lady's man.

Atatürk would have noticed Ebru's entrance. Her smile and intelligent eyes, hinting at her Greek ancestry, charge the room with energy. A successful architect, she is dressed in a black wool beret, Cassock-style button-down coat, and high-heeled lace-up boots, and she reminds us of Laura from *Dr. Zhivago*. But her gray microfiber miniskirt and black tights are definitely from the pages of *W* magazine.

She and Levent hand their coats to a waiter. Levent rushes to give us bear hugs and the prerequisite cheek kisses. A diver with the Turkish navy, engaged in submarine deployments and rescues, he is the maritime version of a top gun fighter pilot. His work often takes him to politically sensitive locations. But tonight, in casual jeans and a black pullover, he looks like any sophisticated city dweller.

"Why do you wait so long before coming to see us?" he says. "We miss you too much."

Levent summons a waiter to fetch more vodka. When the drinks arrive, he clinks our glasses and downs his vodka in one hearty gulp. After deliberating with the waiter about various dishes and methods of preparation, he orders appetizers for the table: buckwheat blinis layered with salmon, sour cream, and Caspian caviar.

"With this we must drink pepper vodka," he says when the blinis arrive.

Ebru smiles sweetly at her husband, arching her eyebrows. "If we keep up with Levent, we will be very drunk, I'm afraid," she teases. "But Levent can handle it. He is like Atatürk, a man of great power."

She turns the conversation to her latest architectural project, the restoration of an eighteenth-century *yali*, a wooden summerhouse, along the European side of the Bosporus, and hesitates before bringing up the subject of Habib.

"He's moved into Ayşe's apartment in Bebek," she says, waiting for the words to assimilate into my brain. "I didn't want to tell you over the phone, but I thought you should know."

The news sends a wave of dread through my body. From the moment Habib said hello at Lipsos Bar in Kalkan, I knew we would be together. Later he confessed that he had a sixth sense about me when Orhan told him "Wendy's friend" had arrived to run the Sun Pension and that he had made a point of introducing himself the night Orhan left me alone at the bar.

I never seriously expected our romance to continue, but I always thought we'd remain more than just friends.

"Ayşe never lets Habib out of her sight," Levent chides, bringing me back to reality. "We rarely get to see him."

"She *has* settled him down a little," Ebru adds, in defense of her uncle. "But when I told him you and Joy were coming to Istanbul, he said he'd like to see you."

Levent explains that he's arranged for Habib to meet me tomorrow. The prospect of seeing Habib again thrills and saddens me, and I can't help feeling a twinge of guilt about Ayşe. Still, I rationalize, Habib and I were friends first and foremost, and that is what matters.

After dinner, as if it's another summer night in Kalkan, Levent switches from vodka and orders a round of rakı, Atatürk's favorite drink.

We rap our glasses on the table. Thump. Thump. Thump. Then we raise them in a toast.

"*Şerefe!*" we say. "To Kalkan."

"I'll see you at the Bebek café at three," says Levent, calling from his cell phone.

In need of moral support, I ask Joy to come with me. "Besides, Habib will be disappointed if he doesn't see you," I say.

Next door to the Bebek café, old men in skullcaps shuffle into the neighborhood mosque. When we enter the crowded room, Levent, who is sitting at a table near a potbellied stove, jumps up to greet us.

"I just spoke to Habib," he says, calling over a waiter and ordering tea. "He's on his way."

No sooner does Levent finish his sentence than I look up to see Habib peer into the café window. He waves and saunters in, a rogue with wild hair and a pale blue sweater I remember well draped over his shoulders. Only then do I realize how much I've missed him.

"Merhaba, canım," he says, using the familiar endearment before taking my hands and kissing my cheeks, enveloping me in the soft wool of his sweater. The faint scent of lemon cologne lingers on my scarf when I pull away, bringing with it all the memories of the past summer. He hugs Joy, kisses Levent on each cheek, and slides his chair close to mine. If not for the urban surroundings, we might be back on our barstools at Lycia Beach.

Habib orders tea and asks about our families and friends. Joy wants to know the latest news from Kalkan and tells him that we haven't heard from Wendy since we left.

"You don't know?" he says. "She broke up with Orhan and went to Greece."

"That would make sense," says Joy, her eyes growing thoughtful. "Wendy has close friends in Athens."

"I'm sorry about your friend," says Habib.

"Me, too," says Joy. "She gave up everything for him."

Habib looks at me as if he's making some kind of calculation.

I change the subject, hoping to lighten the mood, telling him about the dervish festival and how afterward we're going to spend a few days in Cappadocia.

Just as quickly, he changes the subject. "Are you hungry?" he asks. "It's early, but I have friends who own a seafood restaurant in Ortaköy."

Joy and Levent glance at each other.

"I'm late for my class," says Levent, pushing his chair back and standing up.

"And I'm expecting a call from Fred at the hotel," adds Joy, letting Levent help her with her coat. "Do you want to share a taxi?"

And just like that, they're gone.

Outside the café, Habib flags down another taxi and instructs the driver to take us to Ortaköy, casually slipping an arm over my shoulder in the back seat. Within minutes, we're walking hand-in-hand through narrow pedestrian passageways past cafés, restaurants, and souvenir shops.

The restaurant faces the slate-blue Bosporus. In summer, tables will be set outside under umbrellas for the crowds of sun seekers wandering by, but today the maître d' leads us to a quiet corner inside the glass-front terrace, where the owner delivers glasses of rakı.

"How is the bluefish today?" asks Habib.

The owner kisses his fingertips to imply perfection.

"We will have it grilled," says Habib, taking my hand, pressing his fingers over mine.

The waiter leaves and returns with plates of white cheese; *patlıcan*, a cold eggplant dish; *cacık*, yogurt with crushed garlic and mint; and honeydew melon.

My head reels from the effects of the rakı, and I catch myself giggling when Habib feeds me roasted eggplant purée with his fork.

When he broaches the subject of Ayşe, I abruptly return to planet Earth.

"I am lucky that she is working today," he says, a little too sheepishly. "Otherwise I don't think I could have seen you."

"Didn't you tell Ayşe you were meeting me?" I ask.

"Ayşe doesn't understand our friendship. She's jealous of other women, especially you."

Before I can ask him why he has let Ayşe believe I am a threat, he adds, "She can read my thoughts and knows how I feel about you. Anyway, I do what I please. After all, she doesn't own me."

He looks out toward the choppy, gray Bosporus.

How *do* you feel about me? I want to ask, but let it go. His words carry an old bravado, a need to be in control of his life. But in his hands, I sense confusion.

He talks about his decision to move into Ayşe's apartment and their trips to Cappadocia, where she has British friends. "She takes care of me, almost like a mother," he adds, so as not to move into forbidden intimate territory.

I had no idea he'd been in Cappadocia and wonder why he didn't pick up on the subject at the café in Bebek. But his dark, usually cheerful eyes are now grave. "You know I don't like complications," he says.

And so I drop the subject.

We talk long after the sun sets, about his daughter, about the hotel in Kalkan and how in a few years he hopes to sell his interest in it to his brother, about my move to the mountains above San Diego and how I've carved out time to write.

"Do you remember the promise we made in Kalkan?" he says, brushing his fingers across my cheek.

I smile, acknowledging our folly. When we are seventy, if we're both single, we will reunite and live together above Kalkan and the sea. I laugh at how I half expected this would be the way our story would end.

By the time we leave the restaurant, a quarter moon has risen above the Bosporus, trailing a silvery wake across the channel. He holds me and I rest my head against his chest as the cab crosses the Galata Bridge to Sultanahmet, where the floodlit minarets of the Blue Mosque pierce the darkness. When the taxi reaches my hotel, we reluctantly let go, neither of us willing to say good-bye.

Joy looks up from her book when I open the door. "What happened?"

"He's made a life with Ayşe," I say, suddenly exhausted.

She sets down her book. "If it puts your mind at ease, I'm very fond of Habib. But I think he would have hurt you if you'd stayed with him, or made demands you can't possibly fulfill."

"It's amazing what the heart wants and the mind knows," I say.

She smiles. "There's a Sufi tradition, the longing of the lover for the beloved. It's a spiritual quest, of course, the heart seeking its true home. But how would our hearts know where to look if we haven't experienced love in the physical world?

"I know it's a minor consolation," she adds, getting up and grabbing her coat from the closet. "But when men leave, you can count on your girlfriends. I have just the thing to cheer you up."

We enter a crystalline, star-filled night and walk in silence through Gülhane Park to the Lale Pudding Shop, a meeting point in the 1960s for hippies on their way to India to seek adventure and find enlightenment. In front of the shop's plate-glass window, three overweight tourists stare at metal trays filled with stuffed peppers, pilaf, and lamb stew. Inside two businessmen read the daily *Cumhuriyet* over coffee.

Fame came to the Pudding Shop not through the good deeds of its owners, who gave food and drink to stranded travelers, but through the 1978 Oliver Stone movie *Midnight Express*, about a real-life American tourist named Billy Hayes who attempted to smuggle hashish out of Turkey and became embroiled in Turkey's prison system.

At the height of the Vietnam War, hippies and drug smugglers traveled through Turkey shuttling hashish and marijuana from Beirut to the West. President Richard Nixon took a stand on drug trafficking by withholding badly needed foreign aid, pressuring Turkey to crack down on its poppy farmers.

Billy Hayes soon learned that Americans who break laws in foreign countries have few or no legal rights and that Turkish prisons were brutal. While sitting outside the Pudding Shop, smoking joints the size of cigars, hearing tales of the market value of drugs back home, Billy came up with the brilliant idea to tape two kilos of hashish to his chest before boarding a plane home. Billy got caught, becoming a cult hero. And for many, the movie *Midnight Express* continues to be Turkey's trademark.

In the 1980s, the city cleaned up Sultanahmet for a growing number of tourists, and the Pudding Shop, once a smoke-filled den packed with stoned hippies waiting to score drugs or hitch a ride east, became a cafeteria-style restaurant catering to locals and tourists.

"What would you like?" asks a friendly man in a green polo shirt.

"*Sütlaç,* lütfen," I say, using the Turkish name for baked milk pudding.

"Ah, you speak Turkish," he says, in English. "Please join me for tea."

He motions a waiter to pull out chairs at a table where his father, one of the restaurant's founders, eats dinner.

His father gestures toward a mirrored wall covered in photos and newspaper articles chronicling the restaurant's history. Among the memorabilia, he points to an article featuring musician Frank Zappa, who loved their chocolate pudding.

"In those days, my father spent so much time trying to keep kids off drugs. When they had no money for food, he gave them pudding." The man translates for his father, who nods his head in agreement.

"They would park their VW minibuses in front of the Blue Mosque and hang out, trading drugs, even selling their blood for money," he adds. "You would not recognize Sultanahmet in those days. There was a place they called the Tent. Can you imagine, a hundred or more kids living on a hotel roof covered only with canvas? When people came into the restaurant looking for their friends, we sent them straight to the Tent."

He waits patiently while his father makes a point, then translates. "They were kids thinking they could change the world, and Istanbul has always welcomed travelers. But they were also naive."

For many young people, Istanbul marked the beginning of an eastern journey in search of personal transformation. But the ousting of the Shah of Iran and the wars that followed closed the travel route through Iran and Afghanistan over the Hindu Kush, making an overland pursuit of nirvana impossible. The hippies went home, got jobs, and now take planes to visit their gurus.

As we read the messages in a photograph of the original bulletin board, posted by travelers who passed through Istanbul during the seventies, I glance at Joy. She's wrapped a red-and-white-checked tasseled scarf around her neck, one she bought in the bazaar this afternoon because the shopkeeper said it was made near the Syrian border.

"I bet we'll get there one day," she had said, smiling at me.

And it hits me. The Pudding Shop ploy has worked. I'm feeling better.

A message on the bulletin board catches my eye.

"BANJO JOE—Couldn't wait any longer. Gone to Katmandu. Love, Sylvie."

Chapter Six

RUMI AND COKE

Listen to the reed how it tells a tale, complaining of separation
Saying: Ever since I was parted from the reed-bed,
My lament has caused man and woman to moan.

—*Jelaluddin Rumi,* Masnevi, *translated by*
Annemarie Schimmel

Joy

Bekir paces in the doorway of the hotel, his breath creating arabesques of steam in the frigid air. On lampposts, neon signs portraying white-robed dervishes, their hands in mid-twirl, announce the annual

Festival of the Whirling Dervishes, celebrating the great mystic and poet Jelaluddin Rumi.

"Oh, my friends," he says, when Angie and I alight from our taxi. "You are here, thanks be to Allah." He touches his fingertips to forehead in blessing.

Before I reach up to embrace him, he grabs Angie and me in a bear hug, his coat enveloping us in the scent of spice and wood smoke.

A group of women in headscarves and long, drab coats, a few covered head to toe in black chadors, avert their eyes when they pass us. Bekir glances at them and links his arms through ours as he brings us into the somber maroon-and-gray lobby.

"I cannot believe I am seeing you with my own eyes," he says, checking his watch. "And I am very sorry to rush you, but we must be at the stadium in fifteen minutes, so you should change quickly. I will wait here."

He pulls two sheer, white muslin headscarves edged in tiny lavender shells from his jacket pocket. "Gifts for you from my mother," he explains. "Konya is a conservative city, and you will be more comfortable wearing these, I think."

Although Angie and I brought headscarves and have them in our suitcases, we didn't think we'd need to wear them for what has been billed as a theatrical event, and officially we're required to wear headscarves only in mosques. But Bekir says that although the secular government doesn't sanction religious events, tonight's dervish ceremony in celebration of Rumi is as much a spiritual gathering as a performance, and headscarves show respect. So, out of respect for our beloved Bekir, we dutifully agree to wear them.

In our room, with its institution-green walls and a single lightbulb hanging from the ceiling, we change out of our jeans; don long skirts, sweaters, and heavy winter coats; and put on the headscarves. Angie goes for a stylish look and drapes the scarf over her head so that her bangs show, drawing the scalloped edges lightly across her neck and tying them at the back. After a few attempts, I give up and knot the ends under my chin.

The headscarf is a strong, visible symbol in the debate between Turkey's devout and secular citizens. Our friends who follow founder Kemal Atatürk's secular movement and align themselves with the West consider the idea of covering their heads absurd, backward thinking, and downright subversive. "It may seem like a small thing, but it is the first step toward fundamentalism," our friend Ebru has said.

When Atatürk and his ministers formed the Turkish republic in 1923, they set out to recreate Turkey as a modern nation to be taken seriously by the West, making it illegal for women who work or study in government institutions such as hospitals, universities, and courts to cover their heads.

On the other hand, many Muslims, women and men, claim that if Turkey is a true democracy, the government should allow women the right to wear their headscarves wherever they please. "Some women wear wigs just to cover their heads," a young female student we met in the Grand Bazaar had told us. She voiced an opinion shared by many women we know who say that wearing headscarves frees them to move in public without attracting unwanted male attention, a concept we have difficulty grasping.

We return to the lobby looking as drab as the surroundings. Near the front desk, Bekir talks in an animated voice to a short man with light gray eyes set close together below a high forehead, wearing a tan trench coat. He switches from Turkish to English and introduces us to Mahmut, his old army buddy, our host for the evening.

"I cannot tell you how honored I am that you have made the long journey to the festival of Mevlana," says Mahmut, using Rumi's Turkish moniker, Mevlana, "the master." "Mevlana is the greatest of lovers," he adds, explaining that dervishes who devote their lives to God are called lovers and that God represents the beloved, a force so strong that the pain of separation can end only through meditation and prayer.

Mahmut opens the door to the backseat of his car, and we slide in, gripping the headrests when he swerves into an alley before joining a throng of cars filing into the parking lot of Şehir Stadium, the only venue large enough to hold the crowds who come from every province in Turkey.

Bundled in heavy coats against the bitter night air, people press through the entrance and swarm the concession stalls, where hawkers sell souvenirs: fake gold pendants, rings, and bracelets representing ecstatic dervishes in tall conical hats; drawings of Mevlana sitting in meditative repose on a cushion; CDs and books of Rumi's poems. At one table, would-be dervishes try on felt dervish hats and soft, black leather boots.

Inside the stadium, the well-dressed wives of visiting dignitaries look like rare enchanted birds with their lustrous, well-groomed manes of hair and colorful suits, while Angie and I, in coats buttoned to our necks and scarves flattening our hair, look as if we've just trudged across the Anatolian plateau.

We find our seats on the first level above the polished floor of the basketball arena. Behind us, a grandmother swaddled in a maroon coat tucks strands of white hair in place beneath her headscarf. She adjusts the fabric tightly across her brow before unwrapping sesame pastries from a square of cheesecloth, doling out the sweets to three boisterous grandchildren.

Eager to educate us about the dervishes, Mahmut shares the story of Rumi, whom he continues to call Mevlana. One day while Mevlana was walking through the gold market in Konya, he stopped to watch a goldsmith crafting a bracelet. As the goldsmith's hammer rang against the pure metal, Mevlana heard a sound rising toward heaven, answered by a voice calling from the blue sky. He looked up and felt divine light pour through him, seizing him with a love of God so fierce he began to dance.

"There are women dervishes, too," says Mahmut. "But according to Islamic law, they turned separately from the men, and you would never see them in public."

The lights in the stadium flicker. Snacks are packed away, crumbs are brushed from laps, and the audience grows silent. Camera lights pan to the stage, where dignitaries, politicians, and generals from Istanbul and Ankara rise to give speeches and read passages from the Qur'an, to hearty applause.

When a highly decorated general elicits shouts and boos, Bekir leans toward me and explains, "He is trying to make this a political event. The dervish ceremony is very sacred, and he should not do this."

When the speeches end, lights dim, and orchestra members file from the sideline carrying drums, lutes, and violins and take seats at the far end of the basketball court. A choir joins them, ten men in black suits. A tall, thin man steps into the spotlight and begins to chant the opening verse of the Qur'an. "La ilaha Illa 'Llah," he sings.

Bekir leans toward me again. "He's a very famous singer of dervish music," he whispers loud enough for Angie to hear, causing the old woman behind us to silence him with a stern click of her tongue.

The high-pitched, ethereal sound of the *ney*, a reed flute, moves in waves through the auditorium, enveloping the singer's voice. The ney's plaintive call conjures up the image of a bird calling its mate; "the reed longing for the riverbed," says Rumi; or the voice of the lover seeking God, the Beloved.

A drum's steady rhythm answers the ney, striking deep and low like a primal heartbeat. Lush chords of a lute meld with the higher notes of a three-string *kemençe* in counterpoint to the drumbeat. The voice of the ney, meant to silence the material world, seeps into our consciousness, undulating through our bodies. Even the fidgety children behind us become still.

Like apparitions, the dervishes glide through a purplish light onto the court behind their teacher, the sheikh, who wears a green robe and turban, representing the color of Islam. The dervishes, dressed in black robes meant to symbolize their spiritual tombs and tall, camel-hair felt hats representing the ego's tombstone, prepare to dance.

The sheikh stands on a red-dyed sheepskin, symbolizing the earth and all living creatures, and waits for the dervishes to remove their robes to reveal pristine white jackets above full white skirts.

Music swirls through the arena; the drumbeat increases as the choir chants softly. One by one, the dervishes close their eyes, tilt their heads toward their left shoulders, and unfold their arms like elegant flower petals. Their right palms reach toward heaven, their left palms toward the ground. In soft leather slippers, they begin a counterclockwise turn, their hearts becoming the center point of contemplation and their bodies the connection between God and earth.

"They are repeating a chant to themselves," whispers Mahmut. 'We take from God and give to man, spreading grace to earth.'

I've spent many years practicing meditation, sitting on cushions in studios and ashrams, breathing my mind to a still point. But I long to join the dervishes, to feel my body turning on its own axis as my mind rests in ecstatic stillness between heaven and earth.

"*Hu*," the choir exhales the breath of God. "*Hu*," and the dervishes go on turning.

The drumbeat draws us into a ritual that unfolds in three full revolutions around the perimeter of the floor. In the first turning, the dervishes establish a connection with God. In the second, they move deeper into meditation, into their space between heaven and earth. By the third turn, they become planets, part of the universe, and the sheikh becomes the light-giving sun.

The drum and ney sing to each other, and the dervishes' skirts billow like clouds. Eyes closed, the dervishes move as though they are single atoms creating an interlinking field of energy. Not a single unfurled skirt touches another.

The beat of the drum increases, the chanting grows faster, but the dancers have retreated into the calm beauty of turning.

The sheikh discreetly taps a dervish on the shoulder. The dervish gradually slows his pace and moves to the edge of the court. One by one the dervishes slow their pace and stop.

A final prayer from the Qur'an ends in a collective exhalation, "*Hu*," and the breath of God becomes silent. The dervishes pick up their robes, slip them over their shoulders, and follow the sheikh from the arena.

Lights go up, but no one in the audience moves. The dignitaries rise first, breaking the spell. Cell phones ring, families chatter as they gather their belongings. The grandmother seated behind us has already herded her grandchildren toward the lobby.

Beneath a December sky, we untie our scarves and let them fall to our shoulders. Cold air pricks our scalps as we gaze at the stars, feeling as if we, too, have entered the center of the universe.

Under the harsh fluorescent lights of a *çorba lokantası*, a soup restaurant, Angie and I dip spoons into bowls of chicken çorba made with tomato and okra and seasoned with lemon and red pepper. Outside the steamy windows, the thermometer has dipped into the teens, but the soup carries the perfume and warmth of the Mediterranean.

"Mevlana says whatever your religion, whether you are a man or a woman, you are welcome at his table," Mahmut says between sips of tripe çorba.

Sprinkling red pepper flakes into his soup, Mahmut explains how after Kemal Atatürk established the secular republic, he attempted to take away the power of religious mystics by ordering Sufi and dervish sects to disband or face jail sentences.

"The dervishes went underground," he says. "But in recent years, with the approval of the Ministry of Culture, the dervish festival has been sanctioned as a cultural rather than religious event. Mevlana was not only a mystic; he was also a teacher at his father's *medrese*. Students traveled from as far away as India to speak with him and hear the wisdom in his poems and stories. He said that we must live in this world but look to the next as well. And when he died, people of every religion came to Konya to show their respect."

He closes his eyes in reverence as he describes Rumi's tomb, draped in a green carpet with a stone turban at the end, how the tomb sits on a dais beneath the sea-green tiled dome of Konya's Mevlana Museum, housed in a former dervish lodge. Under jewel-colored glass lanterns and crystal chandeliers, pilgrims press close to the carved silver gate surrounding the tomb and offer their prayers.

"Are you a dervish?" I ask.

Mahmut smiles slyly. "No, I make baklava."

"You must see his pastry shop," says Bekir. "We will go there for dessert."

Although it's past ten, we get back into Mahmut's car. He maneuvers through streets congested with festival traffic and turns into a rutted alley, scattering a family of cats whose eyes glow in the headlights. We emerge onto a quiet side street, where he parks the car in front of his shop. Behind a large, plate-glass window bearing the family name in elegant script, we see a backlit case filled with golden baklava, custard pastries, and cookies. Across from the case, a group of men and women sit at a table, sipping tea and watching a game show on a television mounted on a high shelf.

Mahmut brings us past the pastry case and customers through a set of double doors and into the warm, moist heat of the bakery. A man glances up and resumes stretching a thin, translucent sheet of dough across a marble-topped table. Flour drifts into the air, settling over large sacks of nuts and sugar.

"It takes twenty-five sheets of dough to make my baklava," says Mahmut, explaining that his grandfather, a coffee trader, started the bakery business.

"I learned to make baklava from my father twenty years ago, and he learned from his father. It was also my job in the army, where I met Bekir."

"I had *the* most stressful job in all the army," adds Bekir, looking at his friend, who nods in agreement.

Bekir has never mentioned his two-year military service in the Turkish army. With his soft brown eyes and romantic nature, we can't imagine he would have held a dangerous military assignment.

"What did you do?" asks Angie.

"I cared for the pigeons," he says, a look of frustration crossing his eyes.

Unsure whether he is making a joke, we prod him for details.

"The army used the pigeons to carry messages," he says. "But the pigeons were always getting sick. Some died. And whenever I opened their cages, they tried to escape. Believe me, it was terrible."

"Bekir was very good with the birds," adds Mahmut. "Always, they came back to him."

Our image of a fierce Turkish army vanishes. We imagine men caring for birds and dusted up to their toques in flour.

Mahmut's feather-light, syrup-drenched, pistachio-layered baklava melts in my mouth, a revelation when I think of the thick, cloying, baklava I've ordered in many American restaurants.

The assistant baker serves us thimbles of bitter coffee and glasses of water and, when we ask for it, a few more triangles of the delicious dessert before Mahmut and Bekir drop us off at our hotel.

Before Mahmut pulls away, he leans his head out the window and shouts, "Tomorrow you will come to my home for dinner."

Wide awake from caffeine and sugar, we stop for a drink in the hotel lobby. Two men sitting at the opposite end of the room flick ashes from their cigarettes into the air with each point in their conversation.

"We'll have two rakı with water and ice," I say when a waiter holding a black onyx tray comes to take our order.

He nervously grips the edge of his tray. "One moment, please," he says. "I will get Rahim."

A minute later, a young man in an ill-fitting black suit and slicked-back hair walks over to us. The tag pinned to the lapel of his suit says MANAGER.

"I am Rahim," he says. "How may I help you?"

It dawns on us that the hotel Mahmut booked, frequented by Muslim businessmen and families, might not serve alcohol.

"Do you have rakı?" I ask.

Rahim jerks his head upward and clicks his tongue no. Then his face softens, "We have Coke and, of course, tea."

Since the options are either caffeine hot or caffeine cold, we order it in the form of two Cokes.

"*Tamam*, OK," he smiles, and hurries away.

Carrying a silver dish filled with wedges of lemon and an ice bucket, he returns followed by a waiter who sets the drinks on the low table in front of us with a flourish.

"My shift has ended. May I sit down?" the manager asks, and sinks into one of the club chairs. "You are Americans, yes? I would like to practice my English."

Without waiting for our response, he says that he's recently completed the required two years of military service and plans to enroll at the university in Ankara to study chemistry. He asks about our families and seems surprised that we've come to Konya specifically for the dervish festival.

"Why does your husband let you travel alone?" he says, turning to me.

Just before I left for Istanbul, I had attended a dinner party in New York City with Fred. I had been standing with a group of his male colleagues when one of them, a lawyer, asked me the same question. Then, as now, I felt my stomach tense in defensiveness. I give Rahim the answer I gave the lawyer. "Oh, but I let my husband travel alone, too," I say, adding: "Only this time, I am not alone. I'm with Angie."

"It is not good for women to be alone. And *you* have no husband," he says to Angie with a look of sadness in his eyes.

"Mr. Right hasn't come along yet," quips Angie, keeping a light-hearted note in her voice. "But maybe you have an older brother?"

If Rahim got the joke, he doesn't show it. We haven't seen any other foreign tourists in the hotel, so we must seem as exotic as Martians.

The conversation slows and we finish our Cokes, planning to say goodnight, but as soon as we empty our glasses, Rahim orders another round.

"Allah must have called you to the dervish festival," he says, set-. tling into his chair. His voice takes on a bit of gravity when he says he will soon be married and that his future wife wishes to be a lawyer, but he would prefer she stay at home. "A woman should not be a lawyer." He squeezes lemon juice into his Coke. "When she has her monthly time, she cannot control her emotions, and she might ruin the case for her clients."

Angie leans over and accepts the cigarette Rahim offers. When I remind her that she doesn't smoke, she says, "I do tonight," and waits for my response.

"In the States, women lawyers sit on the Supreme Court," I say.

He considers my words before replying, "They are very old, past their childbearing time, and now they have clear judgment."

"But they've practiced law since they were young women," I say, hoping that I'm making some headway.

He finishes his second Coke and looks at our half-empty glasses. Just when we fear he'll order a third round, he checks his watch, thanks us for the conversation, and bids us goodnight.

Back in our room, with its twin beds and stiff, line-dried sheets, we stare at the picture on the pale green wall: A dervish, hands folded in prayer, is painted onto a background of green velvet. Fueled by sugar and caffeine, we give up trying to sleep and read Rumi's poetry until a faint streak of light appears on the horizon.

In the morning, groggy from lack of sleep, we brave a harsh wind blowing from the Russian steppes to meet Bekir and Mahmut at the Iplikçi Mosque and medrese.

"This is a famous mosque, the oldest in Konya," says Mahmut. "The imam is my friend."

On the steps outside the mosque, I remove my shoes, rummage through my backpack, and pull out the headscarf Bekir has given me.

"Guess what I forgot," says Angie, methodically unzipping each compartment of her backpack.

Inside the vestibule, Bekir and Mahmut are deep in conversation with the imam.

"Do you have *anything* I can use?" Angie pleads, running her hand through her hair as if to make the strands vanish. "Rumi taught here, and I can't go inside without covering my head."

I had packed an extra sweater, an orange wool cable knit, in case it was cold in the mosque. Now, I retrieve it from the bottom of my pack and hold it up. "You could wear this," I say, half joking.

"Maybe," says Angie, taking it from me and folding the neckline over to make a straight edge where the shoulders meet the sleeves. She drapes the sweater over her head, knotting the bulky sleeves under her chin. "Does it look OK?" she asks hopefully.

"Rumi would have been pleased to see you make the effort," I say with a rush of affection and admiration.

Mahmut and Bekir politely ignore Angie's makeshift head covering. Inside the mosque, men in dull gray, brown, and black suits have already positioned themselves to face the *mihrab*, a scalloped, pyramid-shaped niche pointing toward Mecca. Bekir brings us to the women's section at the back of the mosque and rejoins Mahmut for the afternoon prayer.

About thirty men kneel on soft carpets, bowing their heads, prostrating to a passage the imam chants from the Qur'an. Meanwhile, we sit alone on an old carpet amid the musty odor of stale socks behind a heavy, dirty brown curtain hanging from a sagging wire.

When the prayers finish, Mahmut introduces the imam, a man in his thirties who is another army buddy. The imam speaks to Mahmut in Turkish and smiles at us, showing even, perfectly white teeth.

"Your respect for our faith pleases the imam," says Mahmut, pointing to our covered heads. "He wants to know if you've thought of becoming Muslims?"

Bekir tilts his head, as surprised by the question as we are, and waits for our answer.

Angie shoots me a glance that says perhaps she went overboard with the sweater.

"It is a big question and one you do not need to answer now," says Mahmut, coming to our rescue. "But my friend thinks you two would make good Muslim women."

The imam's smile hints at infinite patience. "All roads lead to Allah," he says.

In the middle of a treeless block of four-story apartment buildings, with balconies trailing strings of dried peppers and eggplants, Mahmut, Bekir, Angie, and I climb a dimly lit staircase. On the third-floor landing, Mahmut stops in front of a steel door fortified with three locks. Before he can insert a key into the third lock, the door swings open. His wife, Hülya, a dark-haired, petite woman dressed in a tight red sweater and black pants, waits on the other side.

"*Hoşgeldiniz*, welcome," she says, ushering us over the threshold with a warm embrace.

In her early thirties, Hülya—who, according to Mahmut, never leaves home without covering her hair—doesn't seem concerned about wearing a headscarf in her home. She's put on shiny red lip gloss and black eyeliner, and her coal-black hair, cut in a chin-length shag, artfully frames wide cheekbones and marine-blue eyes. Her hands move to create word pictures as she kneels to fit us with house slippers from a shoe rack near the door.

Her ten-year-old daughter, Evren, in a pink T-shirt embroidered with a ballerina in a pink tutu, peers shyly from behind a bedroom door. Evren's eight-year-old brother, Fatih, waits in the kitchen at the end of the hall, his face contorted into an angry grimace that says, "I want my dinner now, and how dare you take my mother's attention away from me."

He lets out a low guttural groan when Hülya ushers us into the living room, where the floor is covered in a beige and green factory-made carpet. A long, low sofa covered in pale rose damask is pushed against the wall and faces a television on a metal stand on the opposite wall. A pile of thin cushions is stacked next to the sofa.

Hülya motions us to sit down while she prepares the tea Mahmut has requested. Evren curls into a corner of the sofa with a coloring book and crayons, while Fatih stalks the room seeking his father's attention. From the kitchen we hear cups clink into saucers and spoons clatter on a tray.

"Does Hülya need help?" I ask.

"Oh no," says Bekir. "You are Hülya's guests. You will insult her if you get up."

Hülya brings in a samovar and tulip-shaped tea glasses, sets them on an end table, and pours tea. She gives us a wistful look, which we acknowledge with one of our own before she goes back to the kitchen.

Fatih, unable to get his mother's attention, stops in front of a birdcage suspended from the ceiling near a window. Inside, a white canary chirps noisily. Fatih reaches up and opens the cage door. Evren shrieks as the bird swoops over the television and lands on Bekir's head. Instinctively, I swat the bird away with the back of my hand. It retreats to a curtain rod, scolding me in a high-pitched staccato.

I feel my cheeks flush with embarrassment.

"Do not worry; this bird is my friend," says Bekir. "He will come back. He always sits on my head."

Bekir lets out a low, sharp whistle and repeats the birdcall until the canary once again perches on his head.

"It is true," says Mahmut, pouring tea. "Bekir talks to him. He can talk to all birds."

Hülya, obviously used to the antics of her husband and his friend, ignores Bekir and the bird. She spreads a white cloth embroidered with fine silk flowers on the floor, orders Evren to set the cushions around it, and rushes back to the kitchen for plates, soup bowls, forks, and napkins.

While we finish our tea, she gives the children their supper in the kitchen. Later, she joins us, urging us to sit cross-legged on the floor while she ferries food from the kitchen. She must have been in the kitchen all day preparing the feast: a traditional soup made with wheat berries and beef broth, topped with yogurt and hot red pepper flakes; sliced green beans sautéed with mint and tomato; and baby eggplants stuffed with minced lamb.

After dinner, ignoring Mahmut's protests, we give Hülya a break and clear the dishes. She leans against her husband's shoulder and sips tea as we gather plates and bowls in our arms.

Angie follows me down the dimly lit hall to the kitchen where we find Faith standing in doorway, his eyes ferocious, his right hand gripping a ten-inch butcher knife, its sharp point leveled at our bellies.

"Put down the knife," I say, nervously backing into Angie.

He stares at us and raises the weapon. I think of a movie I saw as a kid, *Damien*, about a deranged boy—the Antichrist—who had no trouble murdering his elders.

"Put the knife down. Now!" I say, my voice betraying panic.

"Fatih," sings Hülya, meeting us in the hall.

He drops the knife and rushes toward her.

While we regain our breath, she lifts him up, cuddling and caressing him. He burrows his head into her shoulder, squeezing out tears while she whispers endearments. When he quiets down, she sets him on the floor in front of us and says a word. He stands frozen. She says the word again, and again.

The word finally issues forth from his lips. "*Üzgünüm*, I'm sorry," he says, his voice unrepentant, before he runs into his father's arms.

Hülya picks up the knife, a resigned look filling her eyes. She has done her best to honor us by making Fatih apologize, but her world revolves around her firstborn son.

To make amends, she invites us into her kitchen and teaches us how to prepare Turkish coffee. She adds four tablespoons of ground coffee and an equal amount of sugar to a long-handled copper pot, pours in four demitasse cups of water, and sets the pot on her stove to boil. After the mahogany-brown mixture comes to froth, she pours the fragrant drink into tiny gold-rimmed cups.

We wait for Hülya in the kitchen while she serves coffee to Bekir and Mahmut. She returns with a large photo album, which she spreads across the table. There she is in a Turkish schoolgirl's uniform, a blue A-line dress with a Peter Pan collar; in another she's a bride in an elaborate, multilayered, white satin lace gown; and finally, we see a mother holding her newborn son, her husband Mahmut beaming beside her.

Before we leave, she motions us into her bedroom and opens a wooden chest filled with linens from her dowry. Choosing two pieces of cotton cloth embroidered in white silk thread, she reaches across the chasm of language and culture to offer her gifts.

At the door, as we put on our shoes and coats, Evren asks her mother to give us a picture she has drawn of a golden bird flying from his cage and out an open window. You will, too, someday, I think.

"Güle, güle," smiles Mahmut, wishing us a safe journey home.

Fatih holds his mother's hand, looking every inch the adored firstborn son. When we wave good-bye, he flashes his first smile of the evening. She's all mine again, his eyes say.

We're halfway across the hotel lobby when a voice stops us.

"Ladies," calls Rahim from behind the manager's desk. "Wait."

At the elevator, he pushes the button to our floor, holding the door open. "I liked so very much our conversation last night," he says. "I won't see you in the morning, but, Inşallah, I hope you will return to Konya." He holds his right hand to his heart, implying that all good rests in the hands of God.

"Inşallah," we say, pressing our hands to our hearts as the elevator door closes.

No sooner do we put on our pajamas and climb into our beds than a heavy knock rattles the door. I get up and crack it open to find a waiter holding a tray covered with a blue linen hotel napkin.

He glances down both sides of the corridor before stepping inside the room to place the tray on the table between our beds. Lifting the napkin, he reveals two glasses, a small bucket of ice, a water pitcher, and a bowl of pistachios. In the center, taped to a small bottle of rakı, Rahim has attached his business card and written a single word across the front, *Şerefe*, "cheers." Without waiting for a tip, the waiter backs out of the room and quietly closes the door.

A passage from one of Rumi's poems floats through my mind:

> Look! This is love—to fly toward the heavens,
> To tear a hundred veils in ev'ry wink,
> To tear a hundred veils at the beginning . . .

"Şerefe," says Angie.

She places three cubes of ice in each glass, opens the bottle, and pours.

Chapter Seven

ALMOST A HOUSE IN ORTAHISAR

Trust in Allah, but tie your camel.
—Turkish proverb

Angie

Beneath a leaden sky swollen with snowflakes, we hug Bekir good-bye and, with Joy behind the wheel, set out for Cappadocia in our rented Fiat, entering a dreamlike landscape of snow-covered hillocks merging with sky. Time bends, shaped by traces of ancient camel routes, the bark of a Kangal shepherd dog, and the nuance of light as it shifts across the plain.

A convoy of trucks passes by and we imagine instead a caravan of merchants in furs and densely felted robes shepherding carpets woven in Kayseri, bound for Istanbul. On the horizon, the remains of a caravansary rise in a bulwark of ink-dark basalt stone, one of hundreds of former inns across Anatolia that catered to merchants and traders from China, India, Arabia, and the Mediterranean and Black seas.

Built a day's journey apart, caravansaries were a welcome refuge from the harsh Anatolian steppes. There, travelers stopped for the night to water their animals, repair their wagons, and have a meal and a place to sleep.

"This is the route Rumi's family took when they left Afghanistan just ahead of Genghis Kahn and his army," I say to Joy. "There's a good chance they stayed here."

"Let's stop," she says, pulling the car into a small lot.

We enter the caravansary through an arched stone gate into a courtyard where camels once unloaded damask silk, rare pink Persian Gulf pearls, carpets, sable, spices, coffee, and copper and settle under an eave near the former stable. A rich, earthy animal scent permeates the damp enclosure.

"What I wouldn't give for a cup of hot tea," says Joy.

"I'm almost expecting a ghostly tea seller to appear." I shiver and pull my coat collar snug.

"You can almost hear voices," says Joy, lowering her own.

But it's only the wind sighing, "Hu," as it moves through the courtyard.

By the time we find our hotel in Ürgüp, with cavelike rooms carved into a hillside of soft, volcanic tufa stone, the snow has melted. Brushstroke wisps of rose-pink cloud announce the sunset. We check in, eager for a long night's sleep.

Joy and I follow a steep trail that winds like a chalky-white ribbon through ravines and crevices from Ürgüp toward the village of

Göreme. Plateaus meet the horizon before dropping into deep valleys as if sliced open by a sharp, serrated blade. On the horizon, snow covers the dormant volcanic peak of Mount Erciyes, which more than ten thousand years ago spilled lava and ash in layers of soft tufa stone across the Cappadocian plain. Rain and wind have eroded the landscape into *peribacaları*, or "fairy chimneys"—spires rising between houses and churches, some shaped like upside-down cones, others looking like twenty-foot-tall phalluses.

"No wonder you fell in love with Cappadocia," laughs Joy.

"It's been called the Garden of Eden for other reasons," I remind her, which is true. Because the soil is so rich with organic matter, Cappadocia was known throughout the ancient world for the quality of its grapes, apricots, and apples.

"When I was here in August, I hiked in the valleys and found neglected orchards, where I picked apricots that tasted like distilled sunlight," I say. "The owner of a carpet shop befriended me, and I would join him and his workers for lunch. We'd spread newspapers on the floor and share *güveç*, lamb stew cooked in a clay pot, and water *börek* with feta cheese and parsley, made by his mother. They teased me and said they would teach me how to sell carpets. But first they insisted I learn a few more languages. They could negotiate in at least five languages, all acquired from tourists. They also said the most important rule when selling carpets is about trust and friendship. And they shared a secret. If a tourist wants the best price for a carpet, they should visit the shop when it opens, because the first sale of the day belongs to Allah and brings good luck."

We cross a field planted with now-dormant grapevines and climb an escarpment where abandoned Greek troglodyte houses and churches are carved into the hillside. Three crosses representing the Father, Son, and Holy Spirit mark the arched entrance of a cave church, the red paint symbolizing the blood of Christ.

The elusive history of the Orthodox Christians remains tantalizing in these crumbling houses and churches. Until the exchange of populations in 1923, church bells echoed through the valleys alongside the muezzin's call to prayer. Greek and Turkish neighbors became close, sometimes intermarrying, and teaching their children to speak both languages.

"I have a friend on the Greek island of Kos whose grandparents were born here," says Joy. "She described the cave churches and the vineyards as if she knew each and every one, so vivid were the stories her grandparents shared. No one in her family has had the heart to return, although she would like to bring her children one day."

From the courtyard, two slate-colored mourning doves, startled by the melancholy call of the muezzin's noontime prayer, lift into the sky. One by one, chants from village mosques rise and expand over the valley floor. Storm clouds race above the open plain before releasing dense drops of rain on a distant valley. Streaks of lightning slash across the sky. A gust of wind whips up the hems of our coats as we hurry down the hill and take shelter under the corrugated metal roof of a souvenir kiosk lined with miniature polyresin fairy chimneys before hitching a ride from a passing minibus to our hotel in Ürgüp.

By the time the bus drops us off in front of our hotel, coal-dark clouds have drifted east and the sky grows deep blue.

Ahmet, the hotel owner, waves when he sees us walk up the driveway.

"I want to show you something," he calls, and motions toward a cave house he's building on the edge of his property for a friend from Istanbul.

Above the doorway, I notice a cream-colored scorpion embedded in a terracotta tile. When I ask about it, Ahmet explains that the zodiac sign belongs to the owner of the house.

"I'm a Scorpio, too," he says. "She has Armenian blood like me. You would like her and her boyfriend. She's researching our Armenian history. But it is not easy. Of course, some government officials claim that Armenians never lived here. But that is a lie. My grandparents were expelled from Cappadocia in 1915, but before they left, they gave my mother to neighbors who raised her as a Muslim."

He shrugs his shoulders and lifts his hands, palms open. "Allah. God. They are the same to me."

The main room of Ahmet's latest cave house looks similar to the rooms we saw in the abandoned houses on the cliffs above Göreme. Instead of cross motifs and niches for incense holders, there will be skylights, modern plumbing, a kilim-covered sofa, and brass end tables.

"They are so different from each other," says Ahmet, talking about the owners from Istanbul. "He wants to play cards and drink rakı with me. She organizes everything and makes all the decisions. I must find the best rugs and antiques, and she insists I have the house ready by spring. She is demanding but has very good taste."

Already the workers have carved a nook for a television, another for books, and have created a kitchen unlike anything the early Cappadocian cave dwellers could have imagined, with space for a dishwasher and walk-in pantry.

"You see," says Ahmet, tapping the wall, "extra rooms can be added later. You simply dig deeper into the rock wall. Families begin with one or two rooms and carve extra space into the stone when more children arrive."

We tell Ahmet about our morning walk and how last summer I had fallen in love with the Cappadocian light and air and people.

"I wouldn't mind buying a house here," jokes Joy. "It reminds me of villages in Greece, only I can't afford a house in Greece anymore." She smiles as if she's conjuring a memory.

"The houses *are* Greek," says Ahmet, catching himself. "Or were. Why not buy your own Greek house here? Prices are reasonable," he adds. "I have friends in Ortahisar who want to sell. I can take you to see the house tomorrow morning."

When he reveals the price, Joy looks at me. "It couldn't hurt to see it," she says.

Later, tucked under feather duvets in our cave suite, Joy and I discuss the possibility of buying the house.

"I always imagined I would live by the sea," she says. "But something about this place feels right. And maybe my Greek friends would visit."

Perhaps it's an omen: As soon as I fall asleep, I dream of a garden planted with fruit trees, and above the trees a balcony draped with fuchsia bougainvillea, just like our balcony at the Sun Pension.

We wake to a light snowfall. Sparse flakes melt before touching the earth but leave a damp chill. After breakfast, Ahmet drives us to the village of Ortahisar. Patches of snow and ice linger in the shadows of houses built into a rock hill leading to the craggy ruins of a castle perched at the top.

"This place has lovely light even in winter," says Joy, who's now imagining her family settling in for the summer holidays while she peels oranges, pits black olives, and chops parsley for a salad.

Unlike Ürgüp and Göreme, Ortahisar seems devoid of tourists, which makes it even more appealing. Although the castle looks a bit decrepit, we agree that few people can claim a castle as part of their neighborhood. On the corner, in the murky window of an antique shop, copper pots and lanterns totter in haphazard piles. Propped against the window is a large, six-sided copper lantern embedded with red glass beads, reminding me of a lantern I almost bought in Bekir's shop in Kalkan.

"That lantern would be lovely hanging in the entrance of our house," muses Joy.

"So we've bought light fixtures already," I say, and watch her smile.

Beyond a row of houses where peeling pastel blue and green shutters hang on broken hinges, Ahmet stops in front of an ice-covered stone step worn thin by years of use.

"Be careful," he says, struggling with the heavy door, lifting it from its hinges and pushing it open.

Gold-tinged light falls through broken windows in shafts across a splintered wood floor. The living area contains a fireplace built into the far wall. The castle, orchards, and dun-colored plateau appear beyond the kitchen window. We imagine a grandmother tatting lace by the windowsill, where pots of red geraniums tilt toward the sun.

Ignoring the broken plumbing, we see ourselves sitting at our own wooden table. Instead of tatting lace, we'll be tapping at laptops while the scent of apricot, peach, and cherry blossoms wafts into the room from the orchard below.

"A writer's paradise, with only the garden to distract us," says Joy.

"The entire place needs renovation," I say. "We'll be too busy with repairs and painting to write."

Joy's eyes have already wandered toward tufts of weeds and unpruned fruit trees in the yard below, and I can see that she's calculating when she could begin planting a summer garden.

"It sounds crazy," she says. "But we could do this."

"There are two bedrooms, one for each of you, on this level, and you can make another on the floor below," adds Ahmet, enjoying his role as our Cappadocian real-estate agent.

"We can rent the house for part of the year and generate income," I say.

"Yes," says Ahmet. "I promise to find excellent tenants for you. And there is a lady next door who can manage the property."

Soon we're convinced that the purchase of a house is not only a romantic dream but also a practical financial investment.

"Rabia, who looks after some of my properties, has invited you for tea. You will like her."

Down the steps, past a row of olive oil cans that now hold geraniums with a few blood-red blooms, we reach another door, where a stout woman in her midforties waits in black pants, white blouse, a long red knit sweater vest, and a black and red flowered headscarf.

"Welcome," says Rabia, ushering us into her living room, a small, arched space with banquettes built into each wall, a picture of pilgrims in white circling the Ka'aba at Mecca above the fireplace, and a thick brown and white patterned kilim on the floor. "I have dreamed of having neighbors like you," she says. Her ruddy cheeks break into dimples and her eyes crinkle at the corners.

Ahmet takes a call from one of his workers and says that if we wish to stay for tea, he will return in half an hour.

Rabia doesn't wait for our answer. She shoos Ahmet out the door and brings us into her small kitchen, where she prepares tea over a propane stove. The first thing we notice is a photograph placed in the center of a bay window above the sink. Within the gilt frame, Rabia poses beside her front door, flanked by two young men in jeans and sweatshirts, one with her dimples and the other with a longer, more serious face.

She touches the glass, caressing the cheek of the dimpled man, who has inherited her deep-set, pebble-gray eyes. "This is my son, Hasan. He is working in a factory in Hamburg, Germany."

Her finger moves across the frame. "And this is Recep. He moved to Australia to be with his girlfriend. He hopes to attend school in Sydney. I miss my sons, but there is not so much work for them here—only in tourism, and they do not like this work."

Pausing, she gazes through the window to watch a donkey pull a cart through the street before continuing. "They make one call every week and I tell them, 'If you are happy, you must stay.' But I can't help but worry. I am their mother."

She shares that she spends the winter months sewing and crocheting and that during the summer tourist season, she invites visitors into her home for tea and cake and a chance to buy her work.

"I should have my own tourism business," she says, pulling back a cotton cloth and cutting into a semolina cake resting on a large sheet pan.

She places a square on each of three porcelain plates and nibbles on a crumb. "But I am a divorced woman," she adds, rather proudly. "And this is not so easy."

Since tourist season is long over, I'm guessing the cake has rested beneath its cloth for some time. It's so dry, it's almost impossible to eat without dipping it into the glasses of tea she sets before us.

"I shall tell you something," she says, stirring sugar into her tea. "I am the first woman in my family to ask for a divorce. I wanted to do this for many years, but I waited until my sons were grown. Everyone thought I was crazy, but I was not happy with my husband, and he wasn't happy with me. I knew he was with some of the tourist women who came to his pottery shop, so I said to him, 'Go, I am not afraid to live alone.'"

With help from the tea, I manage to swallow some of the cake.

"At first I thought I would sell this house. But the tourist business has been good, and I sell my linens to all of the new foreign owners like you." She cuts three more squares. "My boys love my cake," she says, heaping the grainy golden blocks onto our plates and turning to Joy. "I am so very much looking forward to meeting your daughter. I will make many beautiful linens for her dowry. Just wait one minute and I will get some to show you."

She disappears into the bedroom, and Joy motions for me to look at her bulging coat pocket, stuffed with pieces of cake nestled in a paper napkin.

"There's room for more," she whispers before Rabia returns, carrying linens and dollies in her arms.

Joy picks up a doily crocheted into a delicate, perfect snowflake and holds it up to the light, while I discreetly place my second piece of cake into her coat pocket, leaving one bite on the plate to avoid Rabia's generosity and a third slice.

"My daughter's too young for marriage," says Joy. "But I will buy this for her future. And perhaps someday she will share it with my grandchildren."

"Inşallah, God willing for us both," says Rabia, getting up to answer a knock on the door.

Ahmet joins us in the kitchen and pulls up a chair, wrapping his arms around our shoulders. "I can't wait to phone my friends in Istanbul and tell them that you have found a home."

Rabia takes another plate from her cupboard, cuts a large square of cake, and sets it in front of Ahmet.

"Ah, Rabia," he says. "You make the best cake. Lütfen, please, my dear, would you bring me a glass of tea?"

Later, Joy and I drive to Göreme to visit a carpet shop owned by a British woman who employs local weavers. We enter and find three girls in wool sweaters sitting on low stools behind vertical looms, carefully twisting strands of yarn through the weft.

"May I help you?" says a young woman holding a manila folder stuffed with receipts.

When we tell her we were sent by Rabia, she smiles and invites us inside. "The owner isn't here, but my name is Natalie, and I'm happy to help you. Rabia is a good friend to all of us."

While we wait for tea to arrive, Natalie, more interested in a conversation with her English-speaking visitors than selling carpets, wastes no time in sharing her story.

"I came to Cappadocia on a holiday from Auckland a little over a year ago and fell in love with a Turkish man, a tour guide," she says. "He was attentive, kind, and so sweet. But he had to be away a lot for his job, and he often felt guilty about having sex with me. I mean, it was OK for me to satisfy him, if you know what I mean, but not the other way around. The first time we made love, he leaped out of bed and hurried to the shower to scrub off any trace of my scent. He said he was conflicted between the religious part of his culture, which forbids sex before marriage, and how he felt about me. By the time we broke up, I had made close friends here and decided to stay."

A boy in a white shirt and black pants delivers glasses of orange tea on a brass tray. The sweet tea tastes like hot Tang. Natalie drinks her tea in one gulp and orders another.

"The owner of our shop hires and trains local women to dye yarn and weave so they can keep traditional weaving methods alive," says Natalie. "Many of the other carpet sellers are jealous, but she's so well respected, no one bothers her. We're using wool from local farmers, natural dyes, and the old carpet patterns. You would like her very much, but she's in England at the moment, so I'm watching the shop."

Only when we agree to meet Natalie at an Ürgüp disco to see a belly dancer from nearby Kayseri does she give any indication of breaking the conversation.

The Starlight Disco looks like any other nightclub, except that it's inside a cave. Natalie introduces her friend Mustafa, who clears a path through a crowd of young men and brings us to a table near the stage. The distorted chords of Led Zeppelin's "Black Dog" reverberate against walls and through our bodies.

"Hey, hey mama," sings Natalie along with Robert Plant who wails from a cranked-up amplifier.

"I'm too old for this," Joy shouts after another ear-shattering chord.

"Don't worry," says Mustafa, noticing our distress. "The music will stop for the belly dancer. She only comes here once a month."

We're inclined to make excuses and head back to our room, but beers have been ordered and delivered. Strobe lights flash blue, red, and green on sienna walls and brighten the corner tables, where smoke swirls above the heads of men slouched in lounge chairs. Young and thin, dressed in leather jackets, T-shirts, and jeans, they drape their arms intimately over each other's shoulders.

"Where are the women?" I ask.

Natalie, in a bulky Nordic sweater, whoops out a laugh. "The local families don't want their daughters to mix with Western women. Fear of picking up our wicked ways, I guess."

We follow Natalie's gaze to the dance floor, where two men, dressed like Polo Ralph Lauren models in tight T-shirts and jeans, practice dance moves in front of a wall mirror.

"I swear," says Natalie. "The first month I lived here I thought this was a city of homosexuals. But the men are starved for female affection. Most girls aren't allowed to go out alone, especially to clubs. I can't blame the men for seeking the company of foreign women."

She stubs out her cigarette and continues the conversation we began at the carpet shop. "My boyfriend tried to convert me to Islam so his family would accept me. I covered my head when I visited them, but I couldn't convert. I knew that if I became his wife, he'd expect me to stay home while he continued with his tour groups and met other women."

Natalie looks tired. Stringy brown hair frames her face. Too many cigarettes, glasses of caffeinated tea, and nights inside clubs and bars have turned her complexion sallow.

"Maybe I'll leave after the new year," she says, almost to herself, then sticks a fresh cigarette in her mouth and claps for the dancer, who steps onto the stage, her belly undulating to the music.

Coins woven into a metallic-green belt circling her hips jingle to the drumbeat while she clicks brass zills with her fingertips, drawing us into the spell of her performance. Swirling a gossamer, mint-green scarf from head to neck to breast and waist, she lifts her eyes and tosses back ringlets of hennaed hair, only to drop her gaze forward. Her kohl-rimmed eyes seduce the audience while she covers her face with the gauzy scarf, letting heavy strands of hair fall between her breasts.

She could be one of the priestesses devoted to the mother goddess, Cybele, performing a fertility ritual handed down from woman to woman throughout the Mediterranean and along the trade routes across Anatolia, into Arabia and Persia and on to India. We've often found ourselves awkwardly swinging our hips with our friends in the privacy of their homes.

At intermission, the DJ turns up the amplifier, and Led Zeppelin picks up where it left off. We thank our hosts and slip out of the bar, walking beneath a crescent moon to our quiet cave.

In the morning, when Joy pulls open heavy, velvet curtains, snow-flakes are floating down from the pearl-gray sky like tiny flying carpets. Reluctantly, we pack our bags for the drive to the airport and our flight home for the Christmas holidays. In the breakfast room, the waitress brings coffee while Joy checks her e-mail.

"Fred sent a reply," she says, and reads aloud, "'Deal looks good. Let's discuss when you get home.'" Her voice fills with excitement: "Angie, I think this will happen."

My mind is in high gear. "I'll call my sister when I get home to see if she wants to invest with me. Let's tell Ahmet."

When Ahmet sees us walking toward him and his workmen, he turns his head away.

"I'll bet his Istanbul friends have changed their building plans again," says Joy.

We wait beneath the scorpion plaque above the doorway until he finishes giving instructions to a man mixing plaster. And when we give him our good news, he seems distracted.

"They are forecasting heavy snow," he says. "And the roads can be dangerous, but if you leave now, you should be OK."

His voice has lost its cheerfulness, and he barely makes eye contact.

When I ask if he's spoken to his Istanbul clients, he clears his throat. "Oh, it is such a small world. Ayşe tells me that she knows you."

His voice remains steady. Yet to me, it sounds as if he's speaking in slow motion, making each syllable long and warped. "She says you met her and Habib in Kalkan last summer."

I try to remain calm, but my cheeks burn and my throat goes dry as sandpaper.

"Yes, a small world, indeed," says Joy, stepping in to cover for the shock that must show on my face.

Why hadn't Habib mentioned his plans to build a house with Ayşe when we were together in Istanbul?

"We're ready to make a deposit on the Ortahisar house," says Joy, wanting Ahmet to know that we're still serious homebuyers. "You have our addresses, e-mails, and fax numbers."

Ahmet bends down to brush snow off the tips of his boots.

"My family and I have enjoyed hosting you," he says. "But I'm sorry to say the owners in Ortahisar have decided not to sell their house."

He looks toward the hotel through snow falling in thick, wet flakes, perhaps hoping that one of his staff will rescue him. "I feel bad having given you so much hope."

A sinking feeling settles in my gut, and I don't ask him about other houses.

"What about Rabia?" says Joy, not yet ready to give up. "I told her I would bring my daughter to meet her this summer."

"I am sorry," says Ahmet, giving her a look that says we should not press him. "Rabia will understand."

He squats and picks up a handful of snow, rubbing it between his hands. "The snow is still light, so the main road to the airport will be OK," he says, walking us to the car. "If you drive slowly you will not have any problems."

Joy settles into the passenger seat and unfolds a map while I adjust the driver's seat. For a moment, our rear tires slip and sink into the soft snow. Determined to get us out of town and to the airport on time, Ahmet lodges a piece of cardboard under a rear tire. Suddenly the tire grabs hold.

Harsh winds and snowstorms have thwarted more than one Mongolian and Persian army, but they won't hamper our travels today.

"I'd rather live by the sea anyway," says Joy, smoothing the map across her lap.

"And I vow to swear off Turkish men, go home, and find a nice guy, maybe an engineer from Iowa," I add.

"I won't hold you to that," Joy says with a thoughtful smile.

We drive on in silence, appreciating the stark beauty of the open steppe and marveling at the power of Ayşe to thwart our destiny as cave owners in Cappadocia.

Spring

2003

Chapter Eight

OUR GRAND BASIC
BLACK SEA ADVENTURE

*We got higher into the mountains, and the scenes were most
extravagant and dramatic, and all of us but aunt Dot, who
feared nothing and had great experience, were frightened of
falling off the narrow roads and paths into deep ravines.*

— *Rose Macaulay*, The Towers of Trebizond

Joy

According to legend, in the Kaçkar Mountains above the city of
Trabzon on the Black Sea lived a race of women twice the size of
mere mortals, known as Amazons. Fierce and expert horsewomen,

Amazon women cut off their right breasts so they could better handle bows and the flint-tipped arrows they aimed at their enemies. And an Amazon was allowed to marry only after she killed a man.

To make matters more complicated, in those very same mountains, in an abandoned monastery called Sümela, the Black Madonna, sister of the Amazons and daughter of the Anatolian mother goddess, Cybele, gazes from the dome, her image the symbol of Christianity's feminine ideal, an all-loving mother of the son of God.

When I tell my Greek friend Lili that I am intrigued by the story of the Black Madonna, she reminds me that her grandmother was born in a village near Sümela Monastery.

"Every year," she says, "pilgrims came from all over Anatolia and the Balkans to pray to the Black Madonna."

Like the woman I met years ago on the island of Kos, Lili is curious about her family history, yet hesitant to visit the Black Sea. She connects me with her friends who own a publication called *Greece-in-Print*. A few weeks later, when I receive an assignment to write about the Sümela Monastery, I call Angie.

In the year since we've returned from Cappadocia, we've become more connected to each other and our Turkish friends, especially Bekir and Ebru. During vacations, Angie has visited my family in New Jersey, and I've flown to California to visit her. We've drunk rakı, eaten homemade *mezes*, danced to Turkish pop music, practiced making grilled flatbread, and become experts at frothing Turkish coffee.

Angie suggests that from Trabzon we should go to Ankara to visit the Anatolian Civilizations Museum, which houses one of the world's great collections of artifacts tracing the history of the mother goddess. But before we book our tickets, I discuss my plans with Fred and Sarah.

Thanks to Bekir and the gifts he's sent from his native Gaziantep— a dusty rose kilim for Sarah's bedroom, an antique Syrian Orthodox censor that we've turned into a hanging lamp for the living room, and his mother's prized homemade Antep pepper paste—Fred and Sarah have begun to think of Turkey as my second home.

On an afternoon in February, Sarah calls from school. "Mom, my social studies class is planning to walk out of fourth period to protest the U.S.-led invasion of Iraq. The principal says we might be suspended. Is it OK if I do it?"

For a split second I hesitate, thinking about her academic record. But then I realize I would have done the same thing. "Go ahead," I say, flooded with love for my fifteen-year-old. "If you're suspended, I'll come and get you."

But she isn't suspended, and she returns home flush with her first act of civil disobedience. Because she knows that Turkey shares a border with Iraq, she comes straight into my office to study my map of Turkey.

"Angie and I will be in the Kaçkar Mountains near the headwaters of the Euphrates River in a few weeks," I say, tracing the river's course through Turkey and Syria into Iraq. "One of the Middle East's most important sources of water begins in the land of the Amazons."

"I'll go there with you one day," she says, and wanders out of my office into the kitchen to fix a snack.

Just after dawn on a morning in April, Angie and I board a plane en route from Istanbul to Trabzon. Across the aisle, a young man in a leather jacket helps a very old woman in a robin's-egg-blue tweed coat buckle her seat belt. Immediately they begin a conversation with a middle-age couple in front of them.

Greek spills from their tongues like water splashing over stone and rock. Although my Greek has grown rusty, with a rush of warmth and nostalgia I try to follow the conversation. The young man says something about finding the family home and makes a sharp cutting gesture with the edge of his right palm into his left, emphasizing what seems to be the most important point in the world. The old woman mentions Sümela, but the conversation moves too fast and I lose the thread.

I try to calculate the woman's age. Her silky white hair has been braided and gathered at the nape of her neck. Pale brown eyes remain alert behind thick glasses. Deep wrinkles web her face. If she is a Pontic Greek from the Black Sea region, forced to leave during the 1923 exchange of populations, she is well into her eighties.

After we land, the Greek family pushes into the terminal toward a conveyor belt that is spitting out luggage. "*Afto einai gia mena.* That's mine!" says the older woman. "*Arpazies afto.* Grab it," she calls to the man in the leather jacket. Her voice carries an air of desperation, as if someone might steal her luggage. The man flings their suitcases into a pile.

Angie and I squeeze between two women in dark wool dresses and headscarves and retrieve our bags. We've arranged for a guide with the Turkish Office of Culture and Tourism, and we see him standing on the other side of baggage claim, a man in jeans with a soft pale face and a pear-shaped body beneath his thin, blue windbreaker, holding a sign printed with our names. "Welcome to Trabzon," he calls, his face breaking into a wide smile. "I am Faruk."

He slings my backpack over his shoulder and rolls our luggage to the parking lot, where he introduces his driver, Ömer, who loads our belongings into the back of a Jeep with seats covered in white leopard-print fur.

We settle against the faux fur as Ömer, a tall, quiet man, elegantly maneuvers through a tangle of cars onto a highway constructed as close to the sea as nature will allow.

At open-air markets on what little is left of a neglected beach, women haggle for groceries. Many women wear headscarves, but just as many are uncovered with light hair, hinting at a connection to Georgia and the Caucasus, to the east. Behind the market, the city climbs up a steep hillside in a jumble of tall, half-finished block apartment buildings.

Angie gauges her words carefully and brings up the subject of the Greek tourists and their desire to visit the Sümela Monastery.

"My mother and father were not yet born when all that happened," says Faruk. "But I have met Greeks who come back to look for their family homes."

Faruk doesn't say that he grew up learning an edited version of Turkey's history. After the exchange of Greek and Turkish populations, Kemal Atatürk and his ministers converted the Ottoman-Arabic script into Roman letters, eliminating Greek, Persian, and Arabic words and making it impossible for new generations to read the old texts. They also wrote a revised version of Turkish history, one that began when the Mongol Turk Timur, also known as Tamerlane, invaded Anatolia in the fourteenth century.

Ömer pulls up to the entrance of our hotel, a six-story glass and steel structure with a bustling lobby and atrium lounge. Businessmen and a few businesswomen with briefcases and ringing cell phones sit in oversized chairs and sofas, deep in conversation.

"My friends are eager to meet you," Faruk says after we deposit our luggage in our rooms and return to the lobby. "They own an English-language school and have invited you for supper."

On Maraş *Caddesi*—avenue—we join a crowd of young people in low-slung jeans and denim jackets cruising shops selling Diesel jeans and Dolce&Gabbana knockoffs. Stylish young women have wrapped silky headscarves over top-knotted hair, tying them behind their necks like Grace Kelly ready to take a cruise in Cary Grant's convertible.

Beneath a flashing neon palm tree next to a five-foot-long neon skewer of meat, teenagers gather at the Formica tables of a fast-food joint called Kebab Island. Next door, an equally tall red neon chicken grins and advertises another restaurant, Chickenland. Sidestepping schoolchildren in crisp blue smocks and white Peter Pan collars, we dart down an alley, past shops selling stationery, underwear, and vegetables, and stop in front of a metal door next to a shoe shop.

"Welcome to the Grand Basic School of English," says Faruk.

He swings open the door, turns on a light attached to a timer in the stairwell, and hurries us up the staircase before the light clicks off.

A wiry man dressed in a tan sweater tucked into brown corduroys greets us on the landing.

"Ah, my American teachers," he says, embracing Faruk.

"This is Nuri," says Faruk, his cheeks reddening at our puzzled stares. "One of the owners of the school."

"*Bana mı söylüyorsun?*" says Nuri, pointing an index finger at his chest, his smile set off by flirtatious dimples. "You talkin' to me?"

He bursts into laughter at his dead-on imitation of Robert De Niro in the movie *Taxi Driver*. "Ah, fuhgeddaboudit," he says. "Come and meet Meryem, our head teacher."

Angie shoots me a look that suggests she, too, thinks there's a bigger agenda afoot, but neither of us is sure what it is.

In a small office, Meryem, a statuesque young woman in a lavender turtleneck and black knit pants, rises from behind a wooden desk.

Nuri checks his watch. "Class begins in ten minutes," he says, and darts down the hall.

With a sisterly smile, Meryem motions us to sit on a leather bench across from her desk. "Faruk told us all *aboot* you," she says in an accent straight out of Canada's heartland. "We were hoping you would help teach Nuri's class tonight."

We glance at Faruk, who sits in a chair by the wall, smoking a cigarette. "I think you will enjoy the students," he says sheepishly.

Meryem explains that she's half Canadian and half Turkish. "My mom is from Montreal," she says. "But my dad was born in a village in the mountains outside Trabzon."

Her cheeks flush a delicate rose beneath ink-dark eyes. She practices Islam but was raised Roman Catholic. "Meryem is the Turkish name for Mary, the mother of Jesus," she says. "You will go to Sümela, yes?"

"Of course," says Faruk, when I glance at him.

Meryem tosses her hair over her shoulders with the back of a hand. "Maybe you'll fall in love with this way of life like I have and decide to stay in Trabzon."

A student brings glasses of tea on tiny blue-rimmed saucers. Meryem leans forward and drops two sugar cubes into her glass.

"After college, many of my friends got jobs and moved into apartments," she says. "I was thinking about taking a job in the States, but I didn't want a life where neighbors are strangers. Three years ago I came to visit my father's family for the summer dance festival and met Nuri, who offered me this job."

We expect her to share stories about the culture shock of moving to an eastern Turkish city. But she further surprises us. "I learned something about myself," she says. "I like the closeness of the community here and I believe I can make a difference, especially for the young women who take English classes."

"She's doubled the enrollment of women," says Faruk, finishing his tea.

"Yes," she adds. "We have a waiting list for new students and are looking for more teachers."

She smiles as if to say, "We're looking for teachers just like you."

"Was that a job interview?" Angie says to me an hour later as Faruk brings us into a crowded classroom of thirty advanced English-language students.

"We may have begun new careers," I say, "at least for today."

Faruk leans against a windowsill in the back of the room, looking very happy to have brought us to Nuri and the students.

I smile at a young woman in a pink headscarf sitting in the front row and begin. On a world map against the chalkboard, I point to Wisconsin and Angie points to Michigan. "This is where we were born," I say.

"But where is your family from?" asks a student who sits in front of Faruk.

At first I don't understand.

"Your ancestors, were they born in America?" the student clarifies.

"Oh," smiles Angie, pointing to Poland, Holland, and Germany. "They were born in Europe."

"And my grandparents came from Germany and Poland," I add.

"But I had a Native American great-grandmother who was from the Chippewa tribe in northern Michigan," adds Angie. With her index finger, she traces the state's mittenlike shape, her finger resting on Michigan's border with Canada. "You could say America is like Turkey. We're a mix of many people and cultures."

A number of students raise their hands at the mention of their country.

"What do you think about Turkish food and the Turkish people?" asks a student named Salman.

"The Turkish people are wonderful, and we especially love Turkish food," I say.

"You must try our hamsi, anchovies from the Black Sea," he says. "They are the most delicious fish in the world. There are more recipes to cook hamsi than there are people in Trabzon."

"We know all about hamsi," says Angie, eliciting giggles from the students. "In fact, we hope Faruk will bring us to a restaurant that serves fried hamsi."

Faruk laughs, assuring the class that hamsi is on our agenda.

"If American houses are so big," asks a female student, "why do young people move away from their families before they are married, like Meryem has told us?"

We attempt to explain as best we can that our culture prizes personal independence and encourages young people to live on their own, but none of the students are buying it as a reasonable idea. They say they want to be with their families. Angie and I have spent countless evenings in Turkish homes where the extended family gathers every week.

Halfway through the lesson, Salman again raises his hand. "Your President Abraham Lincoln, he was Turkish, yes?"

Several students banter back and forth in Turkish and repeat the word *Melungeon*.

"Speak in English," says Nuri, who explains that Abraham Lincoln is said to be a Melungeon, which he defines as an American of Turkish descent.

"Elvis Presley was a Melungeon, too," adds Salman.

Our blank expressions lead Nuri to tell us a story. In 1570, after an Ottoman Turkish sailing fleet was destroyed by a band of pirates in the Atlantic Ocean, British Captain Francis Drake captured several hundred Turkish and Portuguese sailors, abandoning them on Roanoke Island in what would become the state of Virginia.

Years later, when the English returned, the sailors had vanished and were said to have assimilated with native tribes and to have moved into Kentucky and Tennessee, where Abraham Lincoln and Elvis Presley were born.

Nuri says the word Melungeon is a corruption of the French word *mélange*, "melting pot," but he also gives an alternate explanation in which the Arabic word *melung* means ill omen and the Turkish word *can* means soul.

"A Melungeon is said to be a lost soul abandoned by Allah," says Nuri. "Meaning one who is lost from their country, family, and religion."

"To be Turkish and become president of America, that is something special, yes?" says a pale, green-eyed young woman named Halide.

"It is," I say. Angie and I have seen many connections between Turkey and America, but we've never heard of this one.

"How many of you want to visit America?" I ask. Since this is an English class, I expect most of the students to raise their hands.

Only two hands go up, both belonging to girls without headscarves, dressed in jeans and sweaters.

"I want to see California," says one of the girls, smiling at Angie. "And maybe learn to surf," she giggles.

Her friend seated next to her laughs and gives her a nudge.

"I am learning English, so I can study your culture," adds the other girl, braiding and unbraiding a length of licorice-black hair. "But I will never go there. I think it is too dangerous. Your president talks of war. And besides, everyone has guns."

We're used to hearing our families and friends warn us to be safe in Turkey, but we've not considered that traveling in the U.S. might seem just as dangerous to these students.

"English is the language of business," says Salman. "But anyway, I think it is impossible for any of us to go to America. It is not so easy to get visas. But I will travel to Britain."

"Or maybe Canada with Meryem," says Halide.

The conversation veers into families, siblings, and fashion. Thirty minutes past the allotted class time, a knock at the door stops the conversation. A man in a bushy sheepskin wig bursts into the room and romps through the aisles, pretending to butt heads with Faruk. We recognize Nuri beneath the wig; he'd slipped out near the end of class.

Laughter erupts. Affection radiates from the students' faces.

"You must stay for supper because tonight we will have music," Meryem says after class. "A kemençe player from the mountains is coming."

She excuses herself and enters a small galley kitchen, where the spicy-sweet scent of tomatoes and peppers wafts from an exhaust fan into the lounge. In a nearby classroom, students spread sheets of newspaper over a long table.

Moments later, she emerges with an oversize, cast-iron skillet steaming with one of our favorite dishes, the pepper, tomato, and egg casserole called *menemen*. Twenty people gather to eat communally, dipping chunks of bread into the mixture.

We've mopped up the last of the sauce when Faruk produces a foil box filled with tissue-thin, syrupy-sweet baklava layered with ground hazelnuts. Just as Meryem finishes describing the merits of baklava made with hazelnuts over the traditional pistachio version, two American students arrive. Redheaded James, loose-limbed and six foot-five, moves like the cartoon character Gumby in baggy jeans. His buddy, Billy, is compact, wiry, and dressed head to toe in black.

James explains that they are from an Arkansas Bible school. "We were handing out pamphlets at the bus station when we met Nuri," he adds with a sly smile.

"We're here to spread the word of Jesus," interrupts Billy. "But Nuri began to teach us some Turkish words. Every week we say it's time to move on, but we've made so many friends."

"Bana mı söylüyorsun?" says Nuri.

"You talkin' to me?" laughs James, scooping up the last piece of baklava.

Halide, who has been following the conversation, jumps in. "Many missionaries have come here," she says. "Everybody trying to convert everybody else, but this is not such an easy place. We have a reputation for being stubborn. Maybe it's our *deli bal*, 'crazy honey.' It is made from a special mountain plant."

"If you taste deli bal," jokes Faruk, "you will dance for days."

"Oh, but it is dangerous," says Halide. "In the villages, they mix it with fresh cow milk. They say you have visions of heaven, but too much will kill you."

"Can we try it?" asks Angie. "I read about deli bal in Rose Macaulay's book *The Towers of Trebizond*." She looks at me and turns back to Faruk. "Do you know where we can get some?"

Faruk nods his head upward and clicks his tongue in a firm dismissive gesture. He turns to greet the kemençe player, who has just arrived, ending further discussion about hallucinogenic honey.

The kemençe player's angular face seems chiseled from the surrounding mountains. He opens a black case, removes a three-stringed instrument, and rests it upright on his knee. The beloved kemençe of the Black Sea looks like a violin that has mated with an eggplant.

Nuri brings an aluminum pot from the kitchen and sits next to the kemençe player, picking up a beat, while Meryem shows us dance steps.

"We call this *horon*," she says.

"Like the Greek *hora*," I say.

With a pang of nostalgia, I remember a night in the *Lefka Ori*, the White Mountains of Crete. Beneath a full moon, men with white handkerchiefs tied over black hair, holding glittering knives between their teeth, taught me the intricate dance steps.

"In our villages," says Faruk, "we dance for harvests and weddings, for making babies, for lost love, for war, for everything. A man will put down his tools and dance when he hears the kemençe."

The kemençe player settles into a tune. Nuri lifts his head and sings words familiar to his students, who join in.

When the song ends and another begins, Nuri sets down his pot, walks over to me, and holds out a hand. I touch his fingertips. We lift our arms above our heads, stepping right foot over left, forward, moving faster as the music accelerates. Faruk brings Angie into the dance. Meryem and several students follow until we form a half circle, moving to the left, up, stomp, and back.

The crowd parts to create a circle around Nuri and James. Nuri leans forward, rolling his shoulders. James lets out a shrill call and ducks under Nuri's arm. Nuri turns to face him and they roll their shoulders, preening like two barnyard roosters. Not to be overlooked, Billy steps in and moonwalks backward, pauses, and performs a series of head-over-heel flips, landing on his knees to raucous applause. I wonder what clever story this pair of missionaries will come up with to explain their "lost" months in Trabzon when they return home.

The beat slows and the dancers fall off until the music stops. Students pick up games of backgammon where they left off or settle in front of the television.

"We must be up early tomorrow," says Faruk, stifling a yawn. "We will visit my friends who have a weaving cooperative in the mountains."

"Oh, you'll meet Aynur," says Meryem, busy collecting tea glasses. "She is a very sweet woman, and even though she is my age, she is from an older generation. You will see what I mean. Please give her my regards."

Ömer parks the car on a steep incline in a village of small cement houses perched on a mountaintop above a valley of poplars and lush tea plantations.

"This is the village of Saka," says Faruk. "It means goldfinch."

We step from the car and are struck by the chuck-clack, chuck-clack of shuttles slapping against wood. Outside a nearby stone and timber house, rows of freshly dyed red and black yarn hang from tree limbs.

A man in a red plaid shirt and baggy jeans waves from the porch of his steep-gabled house.

"*Es Selamün aleyküm*, may peace be upon you, Idris," calls Faruk.

"*Ve aleykümü selam*, and may peace be upon you," replies the man, whom Faruk introduces as Idris Saka.

Idris brings us up an outdoor flight of stairs to a room where two large fly-shuttle looms face each other. Three-foot-wide balls of white, black, yellow, and red yarn hang from ceiling beams and thread through weighted rods to create an intricate, geometric-patterned cloth that reminds us of Navajo and Hopi Indian weavings.

Idris's wife, Aynur, sits at her loom in a crocheted shawl and woven headscarf. She lowers her eyes when we enter, possessing a shyness common among women in villages where Islamic tradition still holds and where women avoid contact with outsiders, especially uncovered foreign women in the company of men.

Her name, which means "moonlight," captivates me, for she seems as illusive as a beam of reflected light. Yet when we share Meryem's greeting, she looks up, her pale gray eyes as curious as our own.

She turns back to her work, and I gaze toward the treadles. Her bare feet press blocks of wood up and down in an even clack, clickety-clack. Flat and wide without arches, her feet have become blocks of flesh that conform to each treadle as if each one is part of a single wooden block.

Glancing at her hands, which deftly turn strands of yarn into sinuous red fabric shot with rows of yellow and black, I want to ask, "Do your feet hurt? How young were you when you started weaving?"

Later, in thick slippers, she shuffles into a small living room to serve tea while Idris talks about the bridge he helped build in Jordan in the years before his village became a weaving cooperative.

Aynur looks up and smiles when Idris says how happy he is now to earn money in Saka village and live at home with his family.

Faruk looks surprised when Angie comments that Idris's surname, Saka, is the same as that of the village. "Did his family found the village?" she asks.

"Everyone from the village has the same surname," explains Faruk, as if this would be obvious. "If I meet someone in Trabzon or Istanbul, or anyone in the world, with the name of Saka, I know they are from here."

Aynur refills our glasses of tea. Her eyes remain downcast as she serves us, but we notice a hint of a smile as she brushes past.

"*Çok teşekkür ederim.* Thank you very much," I say.

"*Bir şey değil.* It's nothing," she says softly, and touches my cheek. Her eyes seek mine, as if to say, "Let's leave the men here. Let's talk about our lives as women."

Idris says something to her, and in that instant, the spell breaks. She gathers the tea glasses. With a glance over her shoulder, she gives us a fleeting smile.

Clouds skitter across the sky above a steel-blue sea. On the horizon, a trawler glides toward the Bosporus and Istanbul. Angie and I sit across from Meryem and Faruk at their favorite seafood restaurant.

"I love our villages for their traditions, but often women are trapped in their homes," says Meryem.

"Aynur isn't trapped," says Faruk.

"That's your opinion," says Meryem. "But you have to admit that in the villages, the man controls his household, even if the woman does most of the work."

"Saka is a village in transition," says Faruk. "You know it will take time."

"True," says Meryem. "But as a school administrator, I must be a role model for the younger women in Trabzon."

Faruk motions a waiter to our table. The restaurant's menu offers countless ways to eat hamsi, the anchovies so dear to our friend Doğan's heart.

Faruk orders from a menu that offers hamsi stuffed, fried, pickled, folded into omelets and cabbage casseroles, and mixed into cornbread.

Talk of women subsides when an anchovy crepe arrives topped with parsley.

Angie spears a piece containing head and fin and gamely chews. "Very tasty," she says. Her voice, filled with sincerity, compels me to follow her example and plunge my fork into the fish-filled crepe.

The crepe tastes salty, crunchy and fishy. "Delicious," I lie.

Faruk leans back in his chair with a grin and offers a basket of hamsi cornbread with little silver fish heads peeking from the grainy yellow squares. He calls over the waiter, who brings a platter of hamsi rolled in cornmeal and deep-fried. This time, the dish is as addictive as french fries.

"You really should stay in Trabzon," Meryem says when we order another basket of fried hamsi.

After dinner, we sip thimblefuls of sweet Turkish coffee and contemplate a new life on the Black Sea. Meryem and Faruk laugh when we suggest that with the money we'll earn teaching English at the Grand Basic School, we'll open our own restaurant, Hamsi Heaven, between Chickenland and Kebab Island, with a glowing neon anchovy gracing the sign and fine coverings woven by Aynur on every table.

Deep in a forest of firs and pine trees, the car slides over a patch of snow and black ice toward a railless edge and gorge before righting itself. After conferring with Ömer, Faruk points across the gorge toward Sümela Monastery, a stone fortress carved into the mountainside and suspended over the deep valley floor.

"We will have to walk from here," says Faruk.

The air hovers just above freezing. Filaments of mist rise from rock and stone. Snow loosens from heavy pine boughs and slips down our necks between scarves and jacket collars. In sunlit tufts through patches of snow, crocuses push slender green shoots holding lavender and yellow buds.

We reach the monastery's main gate and descend a flight of steps into a forlorn courtyard painted with weathered frescoes where, long ago, fanatic Muslims repulsed by images of the human face gouged out the eyes, noses, and lips of apostles, angels, and saints.

From the courtyard, a steady drip of water echoes against the walls of the cave of the Virgin of Sümela, the Black Madonna. Faruk, who has listened patiently to our conversation about faith and gods and goddesses, reminds us that, "Really there is only one God. And here," he adds with a wry smile, "she is a woman."

In her cave sanctuary, twenty feet above our heads, safe from vandals, the Virgin of Sümela, her skin black as night, gazes from the dome, her palms open in blessing. Her son, Jesus, sits on her lap, pressing thumb against ring finger to symbolize the mind's connection to the heart.

I look into her generous eyes and think of the story that brought Angie and me here, of a monk named Barnabas who lived in the monastery of Mount Athos in Greece, how there the monks prayed to an icon of the Virgin Mary said to have been painted by the apostle Luke.

One day, in a vision, the Virgin appeared to Barnabas and told him he would find a cave in the Black Mountains. "You must take my icon and place it there," she said.

And so Barnabas sailed from the Aegean Sea through the Hellespont, into the Sea of Marmara, and up the Bosporus to the Black Sea, where he landed in the Kingdom of Pontus, home of mother Cybele and the Amazons.

"I'll tell you something important now," says Faruk. "You see, the villagers always brought offerings of fruit and grain to this cave and to mother Cybele. When Luke brought the Black Madonna, they treated her as Cybele's sister. Word spread into the valleys of miracles, cures, and answered prayers, and believers from throughout the Byzantine world began to arrive. And after the Ottoman conquest, Muslim pilgrims came, too."

I imagine the monks creating a home for their Virgin Mother, grinding tiny cochineal shells, mixing powder into paint, adding drops of water to precious lapis lazuli to create a cobalt-blue sky, moving in meditation as they painted the ceiling in half-moon strokes.

Outside the cave, late-afternoon sun strikes snow-dusted pines, lighting them like a string of votive candles. Water falls over rock. Muffled voices rise from the icy path. Angie touches my shoulder, and I turn and recognize the blue tweed coat of the woman from our flight.

There are more questions than answers in these mountains. Did the old woman's parents and grandparents dance the horon on the high plateau? Did she lose her family during the exchange when, along with the monks at Sümela, the last of the Pontic Greeks left?

She resolutely makes her way up the icy slope to sit on a ledge in the courtyard and catch her breath in the thin air. The young man squats on his heels and waits.

When we pass by, she looks up with a glint of recognition in her watery, pale gray eyes.

"*Enai oraia edo,*" I say, as the Greek I learned years ago returns to me. "It's beautiful here."

"*Malista Kyria, einai para poli oraia,*" she says with a broad smile. "Yes, it's exceptionally beautiful."

The warmth in her voice is genuine, and yet it's painful to hear Greek spoken in this beautiful, abandoned place.

And while I long to ask questions, she looks at me as if to say, "Please leave me with my memories."

I think of my Greek friend Lili, what her life might have been like had she been born here, had her grandparents and their neighbors not been forced to leave the only homes they knew because of politics and fear. How painful it must have been to open a kitchen cupboard for the last time, to see your garden begin to bloom and to walk past your animals grazing in the field, a gun pointed at your back.

"Joy, Angie," calls Faruk.

He leans down to gather snow with his bare hands and lobs a snowball in our direction. It misses and lands at the feet of the Greek man, who laughs and pitches a snowball back. Faruk ducks beneath a shower of glittery flakes.

Joining the fun, we gather handfuls of soft snow and toss them at Faruk. For a moment, we imagine the monks of Sümela in warm, brown wool robes, succumbing to the temptation of newly fallen snow, casting snowballs across the courtyard. Pilgrims climbing the twisted path would surely have heard their exuberant laughter.

Covered in snow, we bid the Greek woman and her grandson farewell.

When we reach the top of the steps, I turn and see her. Head bowed, she crosses the threshold and disappears into the cave of the Black Virgin.

Chapter Nine

THE QUEEN OF ANATOLIA

Everything we see in the world is
the creative work of women.

—*Mustafa Kemal Atatürk, founder of the Turkish republic*

Joy

The seed of my quest to discover the Divine Mother appeared just before my eighth birthday, on an Easter Sunday on the altar of my mother's Lutheran church. To my dismay, near the altar there was no statue of the Blessed Virgin Mary in her robin's-egg-blue cloak, no snake coiled at her feet. In our Catholic church just across the street, my father's church—into which my mother agreed to baptize my brother, sisters, and me, and which we attended every Sunday, rain or shine—the Blessed Virgin was the Queen of Heaven. For the Lutherans, as far as I could see, there was no queen at all.

Because I loved my mother, who taught me to read, cook, sew, plant seeds in soil, and tend the plants that grew from them, I loved holy Mary, who first and foremost was a mother.

The Easter service ended, and in the weak Midwestern sunshine, my father said something to my mother. She bid her four children farewell and said she would meet us at home.

My dad brushed his hand across his crew cut and said, "Come on, kids. We're going to Mass."

He explained that the Lutheran service we had just attended—with its Holy Ghost instead of Holy Spirit and without Mary, Mother of God, on the altar—did not count in the eyes of our Catholic church.

But everything Mary did, and by extension everything my mother did, counted. Who else packed our lunches? Helped us with our homework? Sewed the yellow Swiss dot Easter dress I wore? It made no sense.

Off we went, across the street and into the sanctuary, where from her alcove Mary gazed upon me with compassionate brown eyes. Why aren't you in my mother's church, I wondered, and felt a seed of doubt settle on my tongue.

Years later, I learned about the Council of Nicaea, a meeting of bishops in 325 CE in what is now Iznik, Turkey, at the request of the first Byzantine Emperor Constantine. There, the Bishops would decide whether Jesus was a man or literally the son of God. The council agreed that Jesus was, indeed, God's son and solidified the Holy Trinity—Father, Son, and Holy Ghost. They also determined that Jesus's mother, Mary, was not a divine being like her son, but only a human woman, impregnated by the grace of a holy messenger. In the debates, schisms, and reformations that followed, Mary was pushed further into the background. I wanted to find out why.

"*An-neh!*"

The little girl's voice vibrates across the courtyard of Ankara's Anatolian Civilizations Museum. In a navy-blue woolen dress and brown tights bunched at her ankles, she tentatively studies our faces, tears shining on her cheeks. "*An-neh!*"

A woman breaks from a group of mothers standing at the ticket booth. In a storm-gray headscarf and black, double-breasted, ankle-length coat, the woman hurries toward her daughter, scolding her indulgently before scooping her into her arms to kiss away the tears.

The call of a lost child seeking her *anne*, her mother, seems a fitting welcome to the museum, which holds one of the world's greatest collections of sculpture and art representing the mother goddess.

Two days before, we had reluctantly said good-bye to Faruk and had driven from Trabzon across the high plain to Ankara, where we await our new guide.

After Faruk and Meryem's warmth and affection, we are utterly unprepared for Dürzü, whom our hotel's concierge claimed was an excellent guide and knowledgeable about the history of the Anatolian mother goddess. In his early thirties, with brown-flecked green eyes and chocolate-brown hair combed back from his forehead, Dürzü has the collegiate good looks capable of seducing unsuspecting females, except for one flaw: his pointy ears make him look like one of Spock's fellow Vulcans, straight out of *Star Trek*. Over the tip of his left ear, a grubby, inch-wide, flesh-colored bandage barely covers a bloody gash.

"I am not only a prrrofesssional guide, I am a sporrrtsman," he says, fingering his ear and rolling his *r*'s for emphasis. "Yesterday we had an important football match. When I challenged a point, the goalkeeper bit me. It was a small fight, but I am full of power, like a bull."

He eyes me flirtatiously and adds, "But today I am *not* a sportsman. I am here to show you the most famous museum in all of Turkey."

Rifling through a packet of smudged, handwritten notes, he blinks his eyes. "I am also very lucky because I am here with two beautiful goddesses."

"In his case, the goddess might decree that he be sacrificed to the greater good of womanhood," Angie whispers as he leads us through the museum, past a replica of a Neolithic wall painting depicting hunters and leopards.

On the main wall in a room reconstructed from the ten-thousand-year-old city of Çatalhöyük, a carving of a woman, her legs spread open and curving upward, appears to be giving birth to three life-size carved heads of bulls that descend from her open legs. I can't help wishing for a glimpse into the minds of our ancestors, who considered the bull to be sacred. For them, the bull was the most powerful animal on land. It could work the fields and provide food, and its large phallus represented unlimited sexual power.

Angie nudges me toward another exhibit where a small figurine of a rotund Bronze Age goddess sits on a throne flanked by two lions.

"Bulls and lions," she says. "The goddess had fierce protectors. I'd love to bring you to Ephesus where you'll see that at the time of Christ, the goddess Artemis was still guarded by lions."

We also notice that throughout the galleries, the spiral appears on statues, pottery, and wall carvings, another symbol outlining the journey from birth to death and the spiritual world. Spirals were painted on earthenware jars shaped like wombs, with long necks to represent the birth canal. The jars held the deceased in a fetal position so that a wife, mother, husband, or child could be born into the world of the spirits.

Among symbols that bear the mark of our collective ancestors who saw the primacy of women in the cycle of life and death we are struck by how much we don't know about human history, and by how deeply ingrained our Western catechism has become, how history goes to those who write it down and preach it.

Dürzu covers his crotch, holding his hands in front of his blue-striped Adidas running pants. "You must know that each spring, young men would cut off their balls and set them on her altar so she could fertilize the fields. She is dangerous, like all women. A man gives a woman his everything," he says in a suddenly hostile voice. "And look what she does. She throws it back in his face."

"Are you serious?" I say.

"You women think you have power over us, but we know better."

A display case to his left holds figurines with full, round buttocks and pendulous breasts, momentarily diverting his attention.

Angie glares at Dürzü. "What is going on with him?" she says to me.

"I don't know," I say. "He doesn't seem to be very fond of women."

When he turns from the case, he's composed himself and his mood has shifted. "I have some special words for you," he says, leaning against the case and winking at me. "It is from a poem called *The Joy of Sumer* and is about a goddess who was called Inanna in Mesopotamia."

From his pack of forlorn notes, he pulls a pale blue envelope containing a badly creased letter. Faded black ink bleeds through the thin sheet. He reads a passage:

My lady looks in sweet wonder from heaven.
The people of Sumer parade before the holy Inanna.
The Lady, who ascends into the heavens, Inanna is radiant.
Mighty, majestic, radiant, and ever youthful.
To you, Inanna, I sing!

"My girlfriend wrote this for me," he says.

"That's a small piece from one of the hymns to Inanna, the great mother of Mesopotamia," I say, recognizing the poem.

"Yes, you know it then." His eyes blink in a nervous tick. "My girlfriend wrote this because we were in love. I don't understand why she left."

"Your girlfriend may have been more serious about Mesopotamian and Sumerian history than you are," I say, wondering how we're going to get through the day with him.

In the courtyard, Dürzü waves to his driver, Ekrem, who impatiently honks his horn.

"Now I will take you to Monument Hill to see Turkey's memorial to our modern-day god," he says. "The mausoleum of the founder of our republic, Mustafa Kemal Atatürk."

At the top of Ankara's Monument Hill, Dürzü stops to catch his breath and light a cigarette. The hill overlooks Ankara, where high-rise buildings and apartment complexes spread into the tawny plain like the edges of an ever-growing amoeba.

Dürzü sweeps his arm toward an eighty-foot-long limestone frieze leading to Atatürk's mausoleum. Carved in boxy relief, women, men, and children wearing heavy boots, headscarves, and thick coats surround a virile Atatürk. With a cape draped over one shoulder, Atatürk knits his brow and extends an arm toward Turkey's future.

The dramatic, twenty-foot-tall, block-cut version of a superhuman Atatürk certainly adds to his myth. There would be no Turkish republic without him, yet his story and rise to power embodies an imperfect communion between Ottoman Islam and secular Western society.

Born in 1881 into a pious Muslim household in cosmopolitan and ethnically mixed Salonika, Greece, Atatürk was exposed early to Western thought and philosophy. His mother gave him a *gobek ismi*, or "belly name"—a special name whispered into a child's ear when the umbilical cord is cut. She called him Mustafa, "chosen one." Later, in primary school, his teacher gave him the name he would use in public, Kemal, meaning "perfection."

Like many educated young men of his generation, Atatürk mistrusted religion and the holy men who preached its doctrine. Influenced by French political philosophy, he believed that to serve his country he would have to rise above God and religion in order to create a republic. This meant an overthrow of the sultan, who represented Islamic Sharia, God's Holy Law.

At the entrance to the mausoleum, a guard in a fitted blue dress coat with gold buttons and a white helmet stands motionless, his right hand resting on the butt of his rifle.

Dürzü snaps his fingers in front of the guard, trying to disrupt a focused gaze. "You cannot even make him blink," he says. "Try it."

We're waiting for the guard to break rank and arrest Dürzü for harassment, but the guard doesn't move a muscle.

"You don't understand," says Dürzü, acknowledging my cold stare. "I was speaking in an ironical style when I said Atatürk is a god. Yes, he made many reforms. But thanks to him, the military, not the people, controls our government."

His eyes grow hard. "Yes," he whispers. "Atatürk was a great man."

A visiting dignitary has left a wreath of red and white carnations near the eternal flame burning in the center of a marble platform above Atatürk's tomb. Dürzü reveals an intriguing fact. Beneath the tomb of the father of modern Turkey is a Phrygian necropolis dedicated to Cybele. Atatürk surely knew this, and we imagine he would have been pleased with the connection to a powerful goddess.

Under his leadership, women gained a level of freedom not attained in much of the West at the time. He created a universal education system that included girls as well as boys. He gave women the right to vote and encouraged them to leave the shelter of their homes to participate in public life alongside their husbands. And influenced by Western women who left their hair uncovered, he abolished the veil in government-run institutions, especially the parliament and schools.

In a small museum exhibiting memorabilia from Atatürk's personal life—finely cut woolen tuxedos with thin silk lapels, an ankle-length cashmere evening cape, calfskin gloves, and narrow patent-leather shoes—we glimpse the man who still causes women to swoon. His dinnerware is no less elegant. Translucent Meissen china is trimmed in gold. Blown-glass stemware from Bohemia carries his initials.

He also loved rakı. The hero of Gallipoli, whose image graces every public and private building throughout Turkey, died of cirrhosis of the liver at age fifty-eight.

"We are beginning the most important part of our tour," Dürzü responds when we insist on returning to our hotel. "You have not eaten, and I am bringing you to the *best* restaurant in all of Turkey."

The Zenger Pasa Konagi, a restored Ottoman mansion, seems made for mystery, intrigue, and Dürzü. Dark wooden stairs lead to the top-floor restaurant, with its panoramic view of Ankara. The late-Ottoman decor verges on camp. Tapestries, woven in deep reds and blues, tell romantic stories of jewel-clad princes and princesses. A gift shop, set up to resemble the salon of a wealthy nineteenth-century homeowner, sells embroidered tablecloths, copper pitchers, and brass samovars.

Dressed as Janissaries from the sultan's army in Aladdin-style gold brocade pants, red cummerbunds, and collarless white shirts, the staff could be on loan from Disney World's Epcot theme park.

Beside a large wooden fireplace, two women in flower-print pants, white blouses, and kerchiefs roll thin layers of dough, stuffing them with mint and feta before cooking them on a heated stone.

"I bring all my best visitors here," says Dürzü, securing a table for four at a window.

A small orchestra consisting of a clarinetist, a percussionist, and an oud player entertains a banquet table of thirty French businessmen and businesswomen and their Turkish counterparts with French ballads.

Ekrem, Dürzü's driver, swaggers over to our table in a trench coat seemingly lifted straight out of Al Capone's closet and takes the seat next to Angie, while Dürzü moves his chair closer to mine.

A waiter arrives. Dürzü and Ekrem order every meze on the menu, beginning with garlicky potato puree, mushrooms in butter sauce, Russian potato salad, eggplant salad, smoked tongue, hard goat cheese flamed in brandy, mixed salad, yogurt with cucumbers, and stuffed grape leaves.

Two bottles of red wine arrive. Dürzü fills glasses to the rim. Ekrem downs his wine in loud gulps and reaches for a bottle.

When I get up to use the restroom, Angie shoots me a look that says, "You had better be quick."

I'm halfway through the dining room when a sweaty hand lands on my shoulder.

"Ah, my beauty," says Dürzü. "I want to show you something when you are finished with your personal business in the ladies' room."

Beyond the restroom door, I hear Dürzü tap his foot impatiently, as if I might turn into a genie and disappear. Were it possible and were Angie not waiting at the table, I might consider the option.

When I open the door, I find Dürzü standing guard with his cell phone in one hand and picking at his bandage with the other. "May I use my phone to take a picture of the lovely lady in front of our beautiful city?" he says. "Believe me, when you get home, you will remember this most important night."

He moves in for a kiss, his breath stale with nicotine. "Oh, you are so beautiful," he says, "Like a *rrrreal* model." He grips my arm. "You can stay with me in Ankara. I will show you so much history. So many goddesses. You will not believe it."

"I'm married," I say, shrugging him off. "And at least ten years older than you."

"But all day you have looked at me with love in your eyes," he says.

"Are you delusional?" I ask, pushing past him into the dining room.

At the table, Angie taps her fingers against her wineglass. Ekrem grins as if he's landed in a romantic fairytale and leans toward her like a stray dog that has found a new home. The band is playing the French national anthem, "La Marseillaise", and, in good humor, the French group sings along, raising glasses of champagne.

Instead of returning to our table, Dürzü stops to speak with a woman in a silk, salmon-colored suit. She nods her head with a knowing smile before pouring a glass of champagne, which he gallantly delivers to me.

Two waiters arrive in fake-fur-edged blue capes and maroon fezzes, carrying a three-foot-long pizza called *lahmacun* on a wooden paddle. A poached egg rests on the minced lamb topping, staring at us like a cyclopean eye.

Ceremoniously, the waiters set the lahmacun on a metal stand high enough to bridge the untouched plates of food below. In staged anger, they withdraw scimitars from their waistbands. One waiter pulls back my neck, the other places his curved knife at my throat, giving Dürzü time to grab my camera and take his prized photograph.

While Dürzü picks at the lahmacun, he turns to Angie and says, "I must tell you something. I am in love with Joy and want to marry with her."

"Don't you think you're a bit late?" says Angie.

A young singer with milky skin and hennaed hair, wearing a forest-green velvet skirt and vest, has joined the band. She sings a tune familiar to her Turkish audience, and Dürzü follows along in a surprisingly lovely tenor. When the song ends, he lunges for my lips. His elbow hits my glass of wine, which lands in my lap, splattering my white cashmere cardigan with red pop-art blotches.

"*Aman. Aman.* Oh, this is terrible," he says, reaching for a napkin.

"Leave me alone," I say, standing up and feeling heartsick at the futility of getting wine stains out of my favorite sweater.

"We'll take the check, please," says Angie, motioning to the waiter.

Dürzü slumps over the lahmacun, head in hand. Ekrem busily refills wineglasses, while I blot the stains with salt and make a compress with my dinner napkin.

For a moment, Dürzü looks at me with a last glimmer of hope. "I am so handsome, yes?" he says. "I feel much electricity and I know you do, too. You must marry with me. I am serious, *rrreally.*"

Ekrem finishes his glass of wine and rises, leaning on the edge of the table to steady himself. Jangling his keys, he tells Dürzü he will get the car.

"Not necessary," says Angie, looking at me. "We'll take a cab."

The waiter delivers a silver-domed platter. With a white-gloved hand, he lifts the lid to reveal the bill.

"Thank you for dinner," says Dürzü, looking away. "They accept all credit cards."

The following morning, we find Dürzü sitting in the hotel breakfast room, dressed in the same sweater and khaki pants he wore the day before, sipping English breakfast tea from a porcelain cup.

We avoid his gaze and take a table on the opposite side of the room, but he picks up his cup and saucer and comes over.

"Today we will tour inside the old city walls," he says. "When shall we begin?"

"Never," says Angie.

For a moment, he looks distraught. "I am so very sorry about your sweater," he says, inching toward me with his teacup. "Please, there is so much more I can show you. We will stop at the bazaar and I will buy for you a new sweater."

"The tour is over," I say.

"OK, ladies." He slams his teacup into its saucer with enough force to slosh amber liquid onto the carpet.

Stunned, we watch him slink out of the lobby.

When we check out of the hotel, we find his order for tea attached to our hotel bill and realize that professional gigolo might be the career that suits him best.

Fall

2005

Chapter Ten

THE EAGLE OF ARARAT

Van in this world, paradise in the next.
—Armenian proverb

Angie

The ferryman steers his skiff across the surface of Lake Van, toward Akdamar Island. In a lustrous wash of color, the alkaline water mirrors a blue-white sky and ripples topaz, reflecting the mountain range surrounding us.

I pencil into my sketchbook the shape of a long-abandoned Armenian church that sits on a rise of a barren hill and for which the island is named.

The manager of our hotel sits cross-legged at the prow and eyes Joy's notebook. Dark brows underscore a high, wide forehead and receding hairline, making him look older than his thirty-four years.

"You are journalists?" he asks when Joy reads aloud a description of the island, which she's just written in fine-point black ink.

"You could say we're writers," she says. "Storytellers more than journalists."

"I write stories, too," he says, motioning us closer and lowering his voice so the ferryman can't hear. "But trust me when I tell you that in Van, the walls have ears."

I look up from my sketchbook.

He glances at the ferryman before lowering his voice to a whisper. "If the authorities see you writing in notebooks they will become suspicious. You must say you are teachers. You see I am Kurdish but also a Turkish citizen. I've been accused of being a terrorist. I am *not*. But if you are Kurdish and live in the east, the authorities suspect you of supporting the PKK."

We've been in Van less than twenty-four hours, but his words echo what our friends in Istanbul have said. They've warned us about the activities and dangers of the Kurdistan Workers Party, or PKK, a separatist organization formed in the early 1970s with the aim of creating a separate Kurdish state.

"The PKK has killed thousands of people, including women and babies," I remember Sami's sister telling me.

When I had asked her about the army's policy of razing any small town or village thought to shelter PKK members, her eyes grew fierce. "What is the army supposed to do?" she said. "The PKK has even trained women to be suicide bombers."

Bekir, too, had expressed concern when we told him we were traveling east before visiting his family in his hometown, Gaziantep. But he had also assured us that the east was stable since the PKK's charismatic leader, Abdullah Öcalan, had been arrested and is now the sole prisoner on İmrali Island near Istanbul.

"We don't see so many tourists in Van," says our guide. "Mostly large groups wanting to see Mount Ararat." He pauses, a faint, curious smile crossing his lips. "I was so surprised to see two American women and wondered, who are you? So be careful. The police may question why you are here."

"If they question us, we've got nothing to hide," says Joy, glancing at me as if to ask, "Why is this man so paranoid?"

"I have been arrested many times only because I am Kurdish," he says, noticing Joy's glance. "I was also in prison, where they tried to make me confess that I was part of the PKK. They used electric prods on my back and sticks to beat the bottoms of my feet. I heard screams from the room next door. They said it was my mother and sister and that they would continue to beat them if I didn't confess. I knew they were lying, but what if it was true?"

He looks away as if he has said too much. "So please," he adds, looking again at our notebooks. "If you write about Van or me, do not use my name."

Joy snaps her journal closed and lets out a long exhale. "We wouldn't want to get you into any trouble," she says.

He stares across the lake toward the mountains. I follow his gaze and see a bird soaring through hard blue light.

"Yes," he says at last. "You may write about me if you wish. But please, call me the Eagle. This is my favorite bird and I think the American symbol of freedom."

When the skiff nears Akdamar Island, the Eagle's face softens. "I wish to tell you a story of this island," he says. "It begins with an Armenian king who built a castle of the finest stone, carved with reliefs of birds and lions and all the creatures of the plain. One morning, his daughter saw a peasant boy tending the island's fruit trees and fell in love with him. He noticed her, too, and each day picked only the ripest fruit for her. Soon they could think of nothing else but each other.

"When the king found out, he grew angry, threatening to kill the boy. But that only made his daughter's love grow stronger. And so, when the moon was new and the sky dark as ink, she hung a lantern in her window. From his hut on the opposite shore, the boy saw the light glimmer and silently rowed his boat across the lake to a grove of cherry trees, where she waited. There, on a bed of velvet moss amongst the sweet-smelling blossoms, they made love.

"But the king's watchman found them and shot an arrow into the boy's heart. The boy died in the arms of his princess. Filled with grief, she refused to eat or drink a drop of liquid. She grew thin and pale as the moonlight itself, and when the next full moon rose, she joined her lover in death. To this day, when the moon is full, you can see the boy's ghost rowing his boat toward the island and a faint glow of lamplight from a shadowy tower."

"He's a romantic," whispers Joy as we gather our journals and slip packs over shoulders.

I watch the Eagle help the ferryman tie the skiff to a post at the edge of a wooden dock. He offers his hand to help us ashore and leads us up a path toward the ruins of an exquisite, imposing church, built in the shape of a cross with a drum turret and conical roof, called the Church of the Holy Cross. It stands in silent testimony to the Armenians who called this part of eastern Turkey their home and who were the first to adopt Christianity as their official religion.

In the interest of full disclosure, I tell the Eagle why we've traveled to Van. In San Diego, I have an older friend whose grandparents were Armenian Christians. In 1918, his extended family was evicted from their homes in Van and forced to walk more than a hundred miles through desert and scrub to Syria. His parents immigrated to the States, but many of his relatives died of dehydration and starvation along the way. He still considers this part of the world his homeland and has campaigned to designate what happened to his family as genocide.

I also share that Joy and I have been surprised by what we've discovered about the region. Armenian history reaches back to the seventh century BCE, when tribes migrated from the east into the area around Van and assimilated with the local population. Ottoman maps from the sixteenth century show Armenian territory spreading from Ankara, in central Anatolia, to the eastern border and into Iran.

"This is a crazy place in so many ways," says the Eagle. "A few years ago, a local official planned to destroy this church and say that no Armenians lived here. But the church has been photographed so often, and so many travelers have written about it. Even he had to agree the idea was stupid. Although no one will say it out loud, everybody knows the Armenians were here as long as anyone can remember.

"Before the First World War, Kurds, Turks, and Armenian Christians all lived as neighbors," he adds. "My grandfather told me what happened when the Russians controlled this region. They encouraged the Armenians to claim the land and separate from Turkey. Local tribes were hired by the sultan to help drive out the Christian Armenians. The sultan said we could keep the land. Of course, all of this happened before the Turkish republic was born. But few Kurdish people will admit or talk about this."

"You *are* talking," says Joy.

He shrugs his shoulders and brings us into the church, his voice rising slightly. "Many people are not educated about history, but I have done much reading. When Adolf Hitler ordered his soldiers to invade Poland and kill every man, woman, and child, he said that no one would stop him. He said, 'Who speaks today of the Armenians?' I think he was right. It is easy for people to forget their own history."

A flock of swallows swoops through the sanctuary and out a high window. The inner church walls show soot and smoke damage. Larger-than-life-size frescoes of holy men stare at us, their long, oval faces and almond-shaped eyes resembling those of the Eagle.

"Someone has to say the truth," he whispers.

The church offers clues into the hearts and skills of Van's Armenian citizens. Carvings on the outside walls tell stories from the Old Testament in vivid block-cut relief. David slays Goliath next to Jonah and the whale. Adam and Eve rise before us, their bellies carved full and round as if both are pregnant. Eve stands with the snake next to the tree of life, her eyes challenging onlookers as if to say, "Who among you wouldn't take a bite from the apple?"

Melancholy overtakes us on the boat ride back to shore. We ask the Eagle to translate the words pressed into the mountainside in bold, white, twenty-foot-high letters.

His voice carries a hint of irony when he reads the words, "I am proud to be a Turk."

"It's nice to have you as my guests," the Eagle says later, relaxing into the cushions set around a brass tea table in the hotel lounge. He orders a round of tea, and we ask him about his family.

"We used to live on our land in the mountain valley on the Iranian border. This was where I was born. My father raised sheep and had horses and donkeys. I loved this life, but during the first Gulf War, when I was a teenager, the government forced our family to move into Van. My parents, sisters, aunts, uncles, and cousins now own an apartment building near this hotel. But my mother hates living in the city. She and my aunts still go to the mountains to spend their summers. You cannot forget that kind of life."

When the tea arrives, he drops a cube of sugar into the glass and watches the granules melt and disappear. "As a child, I listened to many tales of our people. The elders would gather the boys around a fire and tell stories that would last for three nights. The women would do the same with the girls."

"Your English is excellent," I say. "But you seem to have an American accent."

"I taught myself, mostly from books," he explains. "And when I was in the army, they sent me to Izmir, where I worked as a translator for an American officer." A grin crosses his face. "My commander told me I was the best translator on the staff. It was only when he discharged me that he found out I was Kurdish and from Van. He said he was glad he didn't know or he would never have given me the job. I told him Kurds were here before the first Turkish tribes came from central Asia. So really," he says, pleased with his conclusion, "you could say we are native Turks."

We finish our tea in silence. Joy wanders over to a bookshelf in the far corner of the room. She picks out the English translation of Gabriel Garcia Márquez's novel *Love in the Time of Cholera*.

"This is one of my favorites," she says.

"For me," says the Eagle, "I read everything, mostly what tourists leave behind. It is not easy getting these books in Van. I have a collection in my room upstairs. Come, I'll show you."

We take the elevator to the fourth floor. He turns the key in a lock to a room directly above ours and invites us in. Three cinderblock walls are lined with well-worn books whose titles might belong to an advanced literature student. *The Iliad* and *The Odyssey* in Turkish and English share the shelves with English translations of Voltaire and Rousseau, E. M. Forster's short stories, and Joseph Campbell's *The Hero with a Thousand Faces*. On the nightstand a Turkish-English dictionary has been stuffed with sheets of notepaper.

"I like Albert Camus the best," he says, taking a paperback copy of *The Stranger* from the shelf. "In the end, we are all strangers in this world, don't you think?"

"And yet," teases Joy, "in *Love in the Time of Cholera*, Márquez writes about the ultimate triumph of romantic love."

"Yes, it is possible," he says. "This is what I write about, too." He picks up a stack of papers covered with words written in tight cursive and absently thumbs through them.

"I've been writing the story of Akdamar in English," he says. "I would like to show it to you when I am finished." And he bids us good night.

In the morning, a haunting melody weaves through our dreams. We wake to hear the Eagle singing in the shower directly above us. By the time we reach the dining room for breakfast, he waits at a table, his hair wet and slicked back.

"Good morning," he says, making no mention of the shower serenade.

I detect a hint of a wink when he pulls out a chair for me but dismiss the flirtation as wishful thinking on my part.

From the back pocket of his jeans, he withdraws a map and spreads it across the table. Eastern Turkey and Iran appear before us, marked into borders and landmarks and towns.

"I have a surprise today," he smiles. "We are going to Mount Ararat."

Desolate land unfolds in layers of burnished hills until we reach a military checkpoint near the Iranian border. "They are looking for illegal goods and weapons smuggled in from Iran and for Kurds without the proper papers," sighs the Eagle. "They search my car every time I take this road."

He pulls up behind a caravan of dust-covered trucks carrying potatoes and onions within their red-slatted sides. Blue glass eyes hang from rearview mirrors to ward off evil spirits along with emblems that read Maşaallah—Whatever God Wills.

We're next in line and pull up toward the guardhouse, a four-by-four turret of sandbags. The Eagle has been playing a CD of Kurdish music, with its wild calls and ululations, but suddenly he ejects it and shoves it under his seat. The muscles in his jaw clench.

A soldier pokes his head through the Eagle's open window and speaks to him in rapid-fire Turkish. No more than twenty years old, the soldier adjusts the strap of his AK-47 and fingers the trigger, pushing the gun behind his back when the Eagle hands him the identity card all Turkish citizens are required to carry.

"You must give them your passports," says the Eagle. "You will get them back." He slowly gets out of the car and opens the trunk for inspection.

The soldier lifts his aviator-style sunglasses and peers through the window, staring at whatever flesh we have exposed. I pull my scarf over my bare shoulders while Joy, in the backseat, covers her knees with her daypack. Powerless and humiliated, we can only imagine how the Eagle must feel.

"They wanted to check more than our passports," I say after the Eagle gets back in the car and pulls away.

"Because they rarely see American women outside of television," he says.

When the checkpoint fades behind us, he inserts the CD again and cranks up the volume. "They are *salak*, stupid village boys. And tell me, did they think I'd have guns or drugs in my car?" he scoffs.

He shifts into high gear, passing a truck, and drives through a valley of wheat fields and sunflowers tapering off into scruffy hillocks.

"If they had seen this CD, they would have destroyed it." He twists the volume even higher.

"Hai, Hai, Hai!" the voice sings.

"He is calling for freedom," the Eagle shouts.

Speeding along the dusty highway, we join the Eagle: "Hai, Hai, Hai!"

Ishak Pasha Palace rises from a rock ledge nestled into a mountain on the Silk Road heading east into Iran, an amber and cream-colored castle we've seen in dreams and fairytales.

We drive past a boy holding a switch broken from a tree branch, tending a few goats that are grazing among the rocky outcrops. Nearby, in the shade of an olive grove, a family sits on a blanket, eating lunch.

Gusts of hot wind swirl dust at our feet when we step from the car and enter the palace through the main gate. Pulling scarves over our faces to shield noses and mouths from the whirling sand, we cross a courtyard large enough to hold an army.

Built in the seventeenth century, the castle combines Ottoman, Persian, and Seljuk architectural styles and took more than a hundred years to complete. Because it was the administrative center on the eastern frontier, the palace had all the conveniences of its day, including systems for heating, sewage, and water.

From a squat toilet in his chamber, the khan himself could watch for an approaching army. Even so, we can't help thinking how a fortress like Ishak Pasha might have felt like an elegant prison for its inhabitants. In every direction, land disappears into a flat haze, with no indication of life beyond the palace's walls. We can only imagine how Ishak Pasha's wives and daughters, sequestered in the women's chambers and staring at the empty landscape, would long to leave with a nomadic lover.

"Imagine living in this beautiful place and feeling trapped," says Joy.

"No kidding," I say. "I'd escape with the next caravan."

Back in the car, the Eagle turns up the CD player again. A trail of dust obscures the road behind, and we feel as if we're flying.

"I have saved the best for the end of the day," says the Eagle. "Look."

He pulls the car to the side of the road. Across the valley, Mount Ararat floats dreamlike on the horizon, its snow-covered peak glimmering in sunlight. It's not lost on us that historians have found more than seventy thousand separate stories in over seventy languages telling of a god who became displeased with his people and caused a great flood to destroy an evil world.

"You are very lucky," the Eagle says as we get out of the car. "The mountain is always covered in clouds. In Turkish we call it *Ağrı Dağı*, the mountain of pain. It is a dangerous mountain, with crevices and glaciers, and people have died looking for the ark."

Clouds drift past the volcano's snow-covered peak and gather on the horizon. For a moment it becomes completely possible to believe that a man, his wife, and animals two-by-two rested safely on the mountain of pain.

My camera shutter clicks, and the clouds slide back to eclipse the mountain peak. The Eagle checks his watch and informs us that we need to pack up and leave since the area around Ararat is under a five p.m. curfew. Everyone except military personnel must be off the roads until morning.

Ahead, the road splits. One sign points right toward Van, the other left toward Hakkâri, a frontier town near the Iraqi border. In deepening twilight, the land stretches open and empty toward the hills. I long to keep traveling east across the Zagros Mountains to Tabriz and Isfahan. But we turn right and maneuver our way through a flock of sheep ambling down the middle of the road. They skitter to the side only after an insistent honk of the Eagle's horn. Within a few minutes, cinderblock structures appear, announcing the outskirts of Van.

At nine a.m., the temperature already inches toward one hundred degrees Fahrenheit. Despite the heat, we've put on pants, long-sleeved tops, and headscarves and have ventured onto the streets of Van to visit the museum. We might as well be naked for all the attention we're getting. Joy's height and our blond hair peeking out from our scarves attract a group of schoolboys who follow close behind, whispering taunts. When we confront them, they scamper away, giggling.

Little remains of the Van still living in the imaginations and photos of its Armenian citizens, a city that before the final years of the Ottoman Empire was a thriving metropolis of gardens and cafés, where Armenian craftsmen made prized filigreed jewelry. The beautiful homes with tiled floors and gardens filled with fruit and olive trees have been replaced by cheap, utilitarian concrete construction.

Even though Van has the look of a city in survival mode, it possesses a symbol hinting at its inner nature, a statue erected at the city limits. We expect to see modern Turkey's founder, Kemal Atatürk, on horseback, claiming Van as part of the Turkish republic. Or maybe a Soviet-style army tank as homage to Turkey's military might.

But Van's statue, a two-story-tall, snow-white cat indulging a pair of frolicking kittens, catches us off guard. With an eye painted aqua blue and the other sea green, the mother cat stares in benign grace at passersby while a group of boys scramble over her paws and ears.

Later, in the window of a pet store, I see one of the famous Van cats and pull Joy inside. From a row of cages, kittens look up, meowing hopefully and blinking wide green and blue eyes.

"They are the most intelligent of cats and very devoted to their masters," says the pet store owner. "And famous swimmers. They love to dive for fish in Lake Van."

"Remember Roger, the British expat who lived in Kalkan?" says Joy. "He used to walk his Van cat on a leash past Bekir's shop."

I cuddle one of the kittens in my arms. "Of course," I say. "I told him about a cat I had when I was growing up in Michigan, with one blue and one green eye. Roger told me it had to be a Van cat."

Just when I've persuaded Joy to help me bring a kitten back to Istanbul and home, the shopkeeper explains that it's illegal to take Van cats out of Turkey.

I reluctantly hand the kitten back to the owner.

No longer hopeful of being rescued, the kitten stares into our eyes, unblinking, through its metal cage.

A few blocks away in the neglected garden of the Van Museum, a jumble of statues vie for space among the overgrown weeds. Shoots of grass force themselves through cracks in the cement sidewalk that leads to the entrance. A stone ram poised in the center of the garden like a kitschy lawn ornament catches Joy's eye. Labyrinth spirals carved into its sides invite our own mythological theories based on the practices of the mother-worshipping religions that once inhabited the area. "The labyrinth could represent a sacred entrance into the realm of the mother goddess," suggests Joy.

The museum caretaker, in a rumpled suit, looks at us sleepily, as if we've interrupted his midday nap. Scratching his head, he studies the placard on the counter to confirm the admission charge, which is higher for foreigners. He takes our money, hands us tickets, and points toward an arrow leading to the upstairs galleries.

Rooms with dark trim and hardwood floors where an Armenian family once dined, entertained, and slept now house display cases. Most of the artifacts carry lengthy descriptions in Turkish and English hand-typed onto note cards with a manual typewriter, the efforts of a dedicated curator, no doubt. The *e* key has clogged, making the letter appear like a hieroglyph throughout the exhibits.

We peruse the cases of Neolithic tools and pottery and Urartian metal breastplates, swords, helmets, and jewelry. Under the weight of heavy footsteps, the floorboards groan, and we notice the caretaker watching us from the doorway.

Keeping a discreet distance, he follows us up a final flight of stairs to the third floor, where a large yellow sign in heavy black letters says GENOCIDE EXHIBIT.

Our eyes shift to a round glass display case, where three human skeletons lie in a haphazard tangle. A blow to the head has crushed one of the skulls.

"Read this," whispers Joy, moving her fingers along the text on the card. "It says that these remains belong to Turks who were massacred at the hands of Armenians."

We gaze at the bones, ivory-white fingers cupping air, the crushed plates of a skull and the jagged hole where a rifle butt or an axe broke through to the soft tissue inside. Our eyes again focus on the hieroglyphic *e* in the word "Armenian."

Turning our backs on the guard, we descend the creaky stairs of this abandoned Armenian house into sunlight.

"Please, let me take you swimming so you can forget these things," the Eagle says when we return from the museum in a gloomy mood. We agree that a dip in Lake Van will, if not lift our spirits, at least act as a form of cleansing.

In the late afternoon, we drive north onto a dirt road and pass through a village on our way to the beach. The road narrows to a mud-packed lane where goats graze in small pens abutting the houses and men squat in doorways, smoking and drinking tea. We pass a woman in a flowered kerchief using the weight of a drop spindle to twist fibers from a pile of wool into long, even strands.

Her toddler, in a calico dress, clings to the loose fabric of her mother's shalwar pants. A group of ragamuffin children with shocks of red hair springing from their heads in tangled mats runs after the car, hurling stones at us. The Eagle speeds up, and they disappear in a swirl of dust.

Outside the village, the road follows the shore of Lake Van. We park the car and cross the stony beach, spreading thin towels from the hotel onto the rocks and stripping off sweat-soaked clothes down to our bathing suits. Lithe as a gymnast, the Eagle runs across pebbles, stopping every so often to show off a handstand before diving into the gleaming water.

By the time we reach the shore, the water has become as translucent as beach glass in the waning light. A few steps in and the bottom drops away. We roll onto our backs and see the first star of the evening glowing on the eastern horizon. Striations of flamingo pink and plum clouds fan the sky's western edge, where the horizon fades to mauve.

The Eagle swims toward us and initiates a splashing contest. Before long the water roils with our attempts to fend off his two-handed waves. Laughing, Joy calls a truce. Back on shore, we lie across our towels, letting the sun-soaked stones warm our backs.

"I used to live a nomadic life with my family," says the Eagle, cradling his head in his hands as he stares into the dusky heavens. "I didn't see a television until we moved to the city. Now I make my living from tourism and can't live without my mobile phone and the Internet. But when I was a child, my father. gave me a tough Turcoman horse, and I trained him like a puppy. I would ride across the plain and know that I was free."

His story sounds idyllic. I imagine myself on horseback, cloaked in yards of flowing silk, riding beside him, but he goes on to describe another reality of village life.

"By the time I turned twenty, my parents expected me to marry one of my cousins," he says. "But after working in the hotel business, I could not do this. I've tried to educate my family that cousins shouldn't marry each other."

"Couldn't you marry someone from another village?" asks Joy.

He sits up. "This is forbidden. The elders don't want to weaken the family bonds. Anyway, how can I marry a village woman who doesn't understand me? I'm used to meeting modern women like you two. I want my wife to be my partner, to share my love of books and poetry, not only to have children."

"I suppose it's impossible to marry a foreign woman," I say, tempted to make a proposal.

"My mother would kill herself," the Eagle says flatly. "She has told this to me. So what can I do?"

He stands up, shrugging off a subject that has no resolution, and combs the beach for stones. He finds smooth, pink marble pebbles and gray volcanic rock striped with white quartz. When he places several stones in my palm, they look like jewels.

By the time we dress and repack our bags, the Milky Way has illuminated the sky with stardust.

"I've finished my Akdamar story," says the Eagle, squeezing my shoulder affectionately. "It does not have a happy ending, of course. But we must balance our happiness with pain. When you return home and read my story to your friends, I hope you will think of me."

Chapter Eleven

ABRAHAM AND THE MERMAID

Oh Sin, O Nanna, glorified one . . . ,
Sin, unique one, who makes bright . . . ,
Who furnishes light for the people.

—*Assyrian prayer to Sin, the moon god*

Joy

"I am so happy to hear you are OK," Bekir's voice crackles through the phone in the lobby of the Eagle's hotel. "My sister is looking forward to seeing you."

The connection between Kalkan and Van fades, along with Bekir's voice, and the line goes dead.

Minutes later, the phone rings at the front desk, and the clerk hands me the receiver. This time the connection is clearer.

"I am in my shop now," says Bekir, slightly out of breath. "I was saying how I told İpek that you and Angie will be in Gaziantep this afternoon. She is so excited."

He recites his sister's phone number, which I dutifully record in my journal.

From the moment we met him, Bekir has shared stories about his family: his uncles and cousins who supply him with the carved metal urns and antiques he sells in his shop, but especially stories of his sisters, İpek and Kovan, who spoiled their youngest brother and taught him how to pick and brine capers, grill lamb shish kebab with herbs, and bake *künefe*, a spun-wheat pastry with thick clotted cream, pistachios, and rosewater syrup.

"In Gaziantep," he has said, "the food is *the* best in all of Turkey. And my sisters are *the* best cooks in the city. You will go and they will teach you."

"Stay where you are. My nephew Ali will pick you up," İpek says when we phone from the bus station.

Ali, whose brown eyes and thick, black lashes resemble those of his Uncle Bekir, embraces us affectionately before whisking us into his Renault. With the bravado that only those too young to believe in mortality possess, he darts around slow-moving trucks, past Fiat, Toyota, and Nissan showrooms and billboards displaying silhouettes of young men and women in straight-leg jeans, dancing and listening to iPods.

We have no idea where we're going or what Bekir's family has planned, and when we ask for a hotel recommendation, Ali abruptly dismisses the idea: "İpek will be hurt if you don't stay at her home. Everything has been arranged."

He parks the car in front of a salmon-colored suburban duplex. A large terrace faces the street, and flamingo-pink roses bloom in clay pots. İpek bursts from the front door to greet us, kissing my cheeks and hugging me with such force that I lose my breath. She is a female version of her brother, with a soft, fleshy body and jet-black hair angling forward against her cheeks in a haircut designed to make her full face appear thinner.

Inhaling the scent of her perfume, a mixture of fruit, flowers, and spice, I relax for the first time in days, happy to be in the company of a confident and beautiful woman so clearly the center of her family.

"Bekir wants to talk to you," says Ali, handing me his cell phone.

"Welcome to our family home. Oh, how I wish to be there," Bekir says wistfully.

İpek snatches the phone, utters a few words, and hands it back to Ali. Apparently finished sharing us with her brother, she ushers Angie and me into the foyer, where the scent of roasting meat and garlic mingles with an astringent-sweet hint of mint.

Off go our shoes onto a rack by the door. Angie pads into the living room in her cotton socks, but İpek gently calls her back, offering a basket of red leather guest slippers. Like Mesopotamian Cinderellas, we try on pair after pair until we find the right fit.

İpek's daughter and Bekir's favorite niece, Tuva, a high school student, joins us in the hall, wearing tight designer jeans and a pink T-shirt that accentuates her lean figure. From her mother she has inherited thick, dark, straight hair that hangs almost to her waist.

"We are preparing a special meal tonight," says Tuva, taking Angie's hand and bringing us into her mother's kitchen, where polished copper pots hang on hooks above the gas stove.

"And we will start with *yayla çorbası*, a yogurt soup we serve in the evening during the Ramadan fast," she says. "It is so delicious. The yogurt comes from a farm nearby, where the goats are fed thyme and mint." From the counter, she picks up a container of tangy, rich, butter-yellow yogurt.

At the kitchen table, Kovan, a pretty young widow, less exuberant than her sister İpek, quietly motions us to help with the soup. She dips her hand into the wooden bowl, pinches off a bit of dough made from chickpea flour, and rolls the mixture between her thumb and forefingers into ovals that look like chickpeas.

"You'd think we could simply put cooked chickpeas into the soup instead of going to all the trouble to grind them into flour, mix up dough, and shape it back into chickpeas," says Angie.

Tuva translates Angie's comments to her mother and aunt, whose faces show equal mixtures of horror and humor. "Oh, but the texture is so much smoother this way," Tuva laughs. "It wouldn't be the same dish at all and would never be served like that."

Although my grandmother taught me how to make farina dumplings by molding the dough between two teaspoons, I'm having trouble rolling delicate, even-shaped chickpea balls between my fingers. Like Angie, I grew up in a big family, where the best socializing took place in the kitchen. While I can't exactly understand what the women are saying, every so often I catch a word or two. Angie and I have bus tickets to the nearby city of Urfa for the following morning, but İpek and Kovan are discussing how they will keep us in Gaziantep and who will host us tomorrow night.

Caught up in the cooking process, Angie has moved to the stove, where İpek shows her how to mix a cup of hot broth into a bowl of yogurt so the yogurt won't curdle when the mixture is stirred into the simmering soup.

"I'd love to stay for a week's worth of cooking lessons," says Angie.

One of Bekir's aunties arrives and puts me in charge of boiling the chickpea dumplings. The delicate yellow balls swirl in hot water, and I think of a story by Jelaluddin Rumi, about a chickpea and cook.

A cook is boiling chickpeas in a large cauldron when one of the chickpeas realizes he will soon be ladled into a bowl and eaten. Frightened, he tries to escape.

With the back of his spoon, the vigilant cook pushes the chickpea into the pot and says, "You think I'm torturing you, but I am not. I'm simply giving you flavor. You have lived in sunshine and grown from the earth, and now your journey continues. You will mingle with cinnamon and cumin and rice and meat and become the lovely vitality of a human being."

Angie laughs with İpek as I scoop up the dumplings with a slotted spoon and add them to the yogurt soup. In a small frying pan, İpek heats a tablespoon of the mildly sweet-spicy red pepper flakes for which Gaziantep is famous and gently stirs olive oil into the flakes.

I tell İpek about how I taught my daughter, Sarah, to make Bekir's recipe for flatbread using a heel of day-old bread, olive oil, flour, and water, about how I hope Sarah has the chance to visit Gaziantep one day. Angie suggests we bring our friends to İpek's kitchen for cooking classes.

"Yes," says İpek. "And your friends will stay with us."

When the soup is ready, İpek sets the pot on a trivet in the center of her formal dining table, where eight family members have gathered. She ladles soup into bowls and drizzles the pepper-and-oil mixture over the top in whimsical shapes.

A feast lines up in dishes and pots across the table: roasted lamb shanks rubbed with mint and glistening with melted fat; çiğ köfte, raw lamb kneaded with bulgur, red pepper, and lemon, shaped and placed on lettuce leaves; a shepherd salad, made of finely chopped hot green peppers, tomatoes, cucumbers, and spring onions and dressed lightly with lemon and oil; potatoes crisped in olive oil and spiced with cumin.

We fall in love with the soup, a perfect balance of tangy yogurt and "beans" that melt in our mouths. We applaud the cooks, who in turn applaud us, making us believe that the meal never would have been so delicious without our help.

Sisters, cousins, and aunties clear the table, placing leftovers in glass dishes, rinsing plates and cutlery and stacking them into the dishwasher, shooing Angie and me onto a low divan in the living room with glasses of rakı.

"A necessary digestive," says İrfan, İpek's husband, making sure our glasses stay filled as he shows examples of his metalwork.

İrfan holds up a twelve-inch metal urn carved with intricate scroll designs and lines from the Qur'an in minute elegant script, with handles that form a snake whose forked tongue is the lip of the urn.

"My uncle never uses a pattern. The designs gather in his head and travel to his hands," says Ali, tracing a line of script along the snake's back. "From the 'cow' sura of our Qur'an," he says, and reads, "'O you who believe! Seek assistance through patience and prayer; surely Allah is with the patient.'

"My uncle also made two urns bigger than me for the Antep bus station and one for Bekir," adds Ali. "You have seen the urn outside Bekir's shop in Kalkan, yes?"

I think of time drifting into hours in the sunlit courtyard in front of Bekir's shop, where Angie, Bekir, and I laughed and gossiped beside a graceful ten-foot-tall urn carved in calligraphy worthy of a sultan's court. I think also of the tourists who watched Bekir tap his own designs onto metal trays and bowls, eagerly parting with their Turkish liras for one of his creations.

The doorbell rings and another aunt arrives with two cousins, Bahar, who is Tuva's age, and four-year-old Azime.

"Now we must dance," laughs Tuva, as she and Bahar roll up the living room carpet. "Little Azime is just learning."

Ali retrieves a small drum from the front hall and beats a rhythm: bum-*ba*-baba, bum-*ba*-baba. His uncles and father sing along in gruff voices between puffs of cigarettes and sips of rakı: "Aman. Aman."

Precocious Azime shimmies across the carpet to the drumbeat, her tiny hips undulating in slow circles. Holding out her arms, she rolls her shoulders and hands, resting fingertips on the back of her neck and seductively lifting her long black hair to the crown of her head. The miniature belly dancer relishes the attention, stopping to pose for her audience as she moves through the room. With an impish smile, she pulls me up and shows me how to roll belly and hips.

"No, like this," says Tuva, jumping up and sinuously moving to the drumbeat. Soon Bahar joins her. Azime grabs Angie's hand and pulls her into the dance along with the cousins and aunts.

"And now, the very best dancer," Ali calls over his drumbeat, to hearty laughter.

İpek glides between Angie and me. Her hips move in supple curves as her shoulders undulate up and back, sending energy into graceful fingertips. She rolls her belly like a priestess of mother goddess Cybele, dancing a fertility ritual handed down from woman to woman throughout the Mediterranean and along the trade routes from Arabia and Persia to India.

We mimic her moves. Our shoulders jerk awkwardly. Our bellies churn all the food we've eaten. We laugh at our folly until we collapse on the divan between İpek and the aunties.

"I feel like visiting royalty," Angie says when we settle into twin beds in Tuva's room.

"It's a shame we can't stay longer," I say.

Safe within İpek's home, my limbs grow heavy and I drift into a dreamless sleep.

In the morning, İpek packs pistachio baklava in wax paper and a block of cheese and olives for our bus trip to Urfa. She looks at us as if we are setting out for a foreign land rather than a city less than one hundred miles away.

"You must stay longer next time," she says. "This is your home now."

An hour into the bus ride from Gaziantep, our driver stops behind a barricade at a checkpoint. We're used to soldiers boarding the bus and barely glancing at us as they check the identity cards of Kurdish passengers. But since the U.S.-led invasion of Iraq, here in eastern Turkey our passports have been checked more often. This time we're singled out and asked to follow an all-business, twenty-something soldier off the bus.

I stuff my camera deep into my pack and zip it closed, thinking of the Eagle and the guards at the checkpoint on the road to Ishak Pasha. My journal is filled with Kurdish words, and I wonder if the guards will find my notes about the PKK.

"Just answer their questions. Don't say anything else," whispers Angie. "I've been through similar situations in Vietnam and Kenya."

Two older soldiers sit at a table, sweating in the one-hundred-degree heat beneath a tan tarp, and take turns flipping through the pages of our passports.

Fine dust particles suspended in the bone-dry air catch in our throats. We notice that the driver has returned to the bus and stands in the doorway, looking impatient and anxious.

"You were in Van?" asks one of the guards.

"Yes," says Angie.

"Who do you know in Van?"

"No one," she lies. "We're tourists and wanted to see Mount Ararat."

"And you are going to Urfa?"

"Yes, to see the cave where the Prophet Abraham was born, and then to Harran," I say, noticing his eyes soften.

What I don't say is that we're following the trail of a Mesopotamian goddess, Atargatis, a river goddess with the body of a fish and the head of a beautiful maiden. Known as the lady of the waters, she ruled over the life-giving streams and tributaries of the Euphrates River.

The young guard, still cradling his rifle, smiles slightly and returns our precious passports. He gazes toward the road, reminding us that the area has a curfew. Any sightseeing trips must end before five.

Back on the bus, we barely have time to sit before the driver takes off in a flurry of dust, clicking off the miles between the checkpoint and Urfa.

We just as quickly forget the interrogation and concentrate on the land surrounding us. For ten thousand years, the road our bus travels, on the western edge of the Fertile Crescent, has led across the plain and south to Sumer, Babylon, Aleppo, Arabia, and into the Persian Gulf, where traders followed the winds to India. Bounded by the Euphrates River, the Fertile Crescent has yielded enough prebiblical and biblical sites to keep scholars and archaeologists busy until the next millennium.

Not far from the city of Urfa, archaeologists discovered tablets from the third millennium BCE that contained the world's first known written epic, the story of Gilgamesh. Two-thirds man, one-third god, Gilgamesh, founder of the city of Uruk, longed for a life of adventure and left his kingdom to befriend Enkidu, the wild man of the forest. Together they vanquished many foes. When the goddess Ishtar, Queen of Heaven, offered herself to Gilgamesh, he rebuffed her and killed her protector, the sacred bull.

As the bus attendant makes his way up the aisle with snacks of tea and cake, Angie and I retrieve our journals from our packs and settle into the journey. I pull out my pen and write: Here is where the story shifts from goddesses and gods and magical animals to a single, all-powerful deity.

Sweat-soaked and as dusty as camel herders, we reach the check-in desk in the air-conditioned lobby of Urfa's Harran Hotel and get in line behind a short, athletic man in his twenties, wearing a well-traveled, green flak jacket.

"Sir," says the desk clerk. "May I see your passport, please?"

The young man shakes unruly black curls, shrugs a large backpack from his shoulders onto the marble floor, and rummages through its contents. Out come shorts, a gray T-shirt, and filthy, unmatched socks.

"I can't find my passport," he mumbles.

"Will you pay with credit card or cash?" says the desk clerk.

"If I pay cash up front, I don't understand why I need to leave my passport," says the young man. He stuffs clothes back into his pack and looks to us for reassurance.

"It's required," I say, irritation oozing from each word. Already I miss the warmth and hospitality of Bekir's family.

"May I call you Abraham?" asks the young man, referring to the nametag on the desk clerk's jacket. Before the clerk can respond, the young man continues, "Abraham, I'll give you twenty-five dollars cash for a single room."

"I'm sorry, but I cannot make such a discount." Abraham gives us an equally pleading glance.

"Then maybe you can help me with a problem," says the young man. "Would you call the police and report what happened at the pension where I stayed last night? The owner gave my room away and left my pack outside the door. Maybe he stole my passport."

"I wouldn't get the police involved," says Angie. "You're only passing through, and they have every reason to side with the pension owner."

"The lady is correct," says Abraham. "It would not be good to contact the police. It will make the problem worse. But I can offer a 10 percent discount for a room," he adds politely. "I will give this discount to the ladies, too."

"OK, maybe you're right." The young man holds out a grimy hand to a more sympathetic Angie. "Hi, I'm Daniel, but here they call me Captain Kebab," he says, explaining that he earned his nickname in a kebab house in Trabzon. "I've been in Turkey for three months. Last night, I invited some Australian girls for drinks in my room, and later we all went out. OK, I admit it. I didn't get back until after two in the morning. The owner left my backpack outside the door and I had to sleep on the street. I'm going home in a week, and I don't want to wire for more money. I'm sure the Aussie ladies will let me crash in their room tonight. But I really have to find my passport."

Captain Kebab removes a rubber band from his wrist and ties his curly hair back into a ponytail, revealing a pale forehead that is in contrast to the rest of his tanned face.

"Listen," he says, pulling notebooks and papers from his backpack's side pockets. "You have to go to Harran. That's where the Prophet Abraham and Sarah stayed before going to the promised land. Abraham's father is buried there. I mean, we're in the land of the Old Testament, the cradle of civilization!"

From the bottom of his pack, he retrieves a bent and worn passport.

"OK, OK," he says, when I give him a "think before you speak" look I often give my daughter. "But the guy kicked me out of my room for no reason."

"It *is* more conservative here," says Angie, in a motherly tone.

Captain Kebab moves aside so that Abraham can take our passports, and asks us where we've traveled in Turkey. When we mention that we've been to Trabzon, Captain Kebab chimes in. "I was there last month and loved it. I met some students at this English-language school and spent an entire week hanging out with them."

"The Grand Basic School of English?" says Angie.

Captain Kebab's eyes widen. "Do you know Nuri and Meryem? I met Nuri at a teahouse where I was playing backgammon. His father is a *hoja*, a scholar, who memorized the entire Qur'an. So has Nuri. His father brought him on the hajj to Mecca. Did you meet James and Billy? At first they tried to convert me, but thanks to Hebrew school, I can quote the Torah in Hebrew. That impressed them."

We invite Captain Kebab to join us for Fantas, and for the next half-hour, we share stories of life at the Grand Basic School of English, presided over by Nuri and Meryem, who, it seems, have chosen to accept everyone.

The following morning, while we're having breakfast, Abraham, the desk clerk, stops by our table in the dining room. "My shift has ended," he says. "Please, I would very much like to take you to the bazaar. I must go home and change, but will meet you in the lobby in half an hour."

We find him pacing the lobby in a short-sleeved, white, button-down shirt and pressed black pants, a pen in his shirt pocket and a notebook in hand. His perfectly chiseled face with a long, straight nose, wide, dark eyes and Cupid's-bow lips has appeared on sculptures we've seen in Turkish museums, an antique face from an Egyptian frieze.

On the wide boulevard in front of the hotel, cars whiz by with little regard for lanes. Businessmen chat on their cell phones, walking through the crowd as if no one but the person they're talking to exists.

Dressed in loose-fitting pants, long-sleeved shirts, and light-colored headscarves, we hold on to Abraham as we cross the boulevard toward Urfa's open-air bazaar.

Considered the fourth-holiest city in Islam, Urfa has two reasons to claim a place in the pantheon of great religious cities. Legend has it that when the Prophet Abraham was a baby, his mother hid him in a cave here. Later, Abraham fought the powerful King Nimrod, who worshipped the moon god Sin. Abraham won and would become the patriarch of three religions: Judaism, Christianity, and Islam.

Urfa was also the first city to officially adopt Christianity, and it is said that Jesus himself corresponded with King Abgar, who ruled at the time.

"Would you like a cigarette?" Abraham asks as we enter the bazaar, a labyrinth of covered streets surrounding a large arcaded square. Beneath a tree, two men pinch copper-colored tobacco from a large bale and expertly roll thin cigarettes, which they sell for a few Turkish liras each. They invite us to sit down, and in less than a minute, glasses of tea arrive and we're offered hand-rolled cigarettes.

A crowd gathers to stare at our light skin and eyes. A woman in a red, ankle-length dress embroidered with silver thread inches forward. She says something to Abraham, who turns to me and translates. "She would like to touch your hair."

I can see that she's young, although her tanned face is lined and she's missing a front tooth. I motion her over and she shyly pets my braided hair. I feel a rush of affection and wish there were a way to communicate with her, especially when I notice blue dots tattooed below her bottom lip, which Abraham explains are tattoos showing that she's married and wife number three of four.

"In our tradition, a husband may have four wives," says Abraham, gazing into his tea. "And if the husband wishes to make room for another, he can ask for a divorce. My father has done this to my mother."

Before he can say more, the woman speaks to him and smiles, and disappears into the crowd.

"She wanted me to tell you that you brought a memory back to her. When her oldest child was a baby, he had hair as golden as yours," says Abraham. "But his hair is now black as the night sky."

The cigarette burns between my fingers, smelling sweet and aromatic. "Tell us about your mother," I say.

Angie moves closer, stubbing her cigarette on the ground. In the arcaded balcony above the bazaar, boys sit at treadle sewing machines and make shirts, bolts of white cotton broadcloth on the floor next to them. The whirring sound drifts through the stalls below.

Abraham raises his eyes toward the balcony as he speaks. "One morning my father was playing football in the street with his friends," he says softly. "Suddenly, my grandmother called to him and said, 'Hamid, you must come home. It is your wedding day.' He cried and said, 'No,' but my grandmother said it was too late; the dowry price of fifteen sheep had already been paid. My father was eleven when he married his first wife, Mira, and she was seventeen. When my father turned eighteen, he married my mother. He has six children with Mira, eight with my mother, and I am my mother's oldest son. His third wife has five children, and his fourth, only two. But now my father will marry another woman and has asked my mother to leave. He cannot ask this of the first wife because she is the most important. It is my responsibility to take care of my mother.

"It's OK," he says, his voice filled with disappointment. "I wanted to go to university to study hotel management. Maybe I will some-day. Inşallah."

We sit quietly and finish our tea. Nothing we might say would alter the bonds holding Abraham to his father and mother.

He collects our tea glasses and motions us past a row of copper smelters and into a lane where we buy purple and fuchsia silk from Aleppo, Syria.

"I will take you to the Sacred Pools of the Prophet Abraham. My mother has named me for him, may peace be upon him," he says, pride filling his voice.

The miracle of the Pools of Abraham has intrigued me since I first learned that the fishtailed goddess, Atargatis, has a connection to the Prophet Abraham.

For thousands of years, in a region where land can turn to dust overnight, Atargatis and her handmaidens, who took the form of fish, ruled over rivers and springs. One such river, the Karakoyun Deresi, flows through Urfa. Known during Byzantine times as Skirtos, the Leaping River, it provided water to the surrounding countryside, making the region a major producer of fruit and vegetables. At times the river overflowed its boundaries, flooding the city and killing thousands of residents. To appease the river, the locals made offerings to Atargatis, recognizing the power she had to nourish and destroy life.

With the rise of Christianity, the image of the fish goddess merged with that of Mary, the virgin mother whose name Stella Maris means Star of the Sea. In Syrian Orthodox Churches, you can find images of Mary wearing her golden, star-tipped crown and sporting a mermaid's tail.

The story connecting the Prophet Abraham to Atargatis also connects them to the pagan King Nimrod who declared himself greater than all the gods. Nimrod consolidated his power between the Tigris and Euphrates Rivers from Mesopotamia to the Persian Gulf. Here he made sacrifices to his gods and goddesses. It is said he was so ambitious, he built the Tower of Babel and tried to reach heaven by constructing the tallest staircase in the world.

When Nimrod learned that a prophet had been born who would one day end his reign and that of his gods, he ordered all the boys in Urfa to be killed. Abraham's mother heard the news and hid her son in a cave below the citadel in Urfa. She had a famous role model, the Greek Goddess Rhea who hid her infant Zeus from his vengeful father Chronos in a cave on the island of Crete.

Abraham's father, Terah, was an idol maker who believed in many gods. Terah worried about his son who heard the voice of a single, all-knowing god, a god who didn't take the form of a statue. Perhaps it was a test, but one day Terah asked Abraham to watch over the idols in his shop while he was away on business.

Staring at the idols, Abraham dared them to speak. "You are false," he said, when they remained silent. "Speak to me or I will smash you."

He picked up his father's hammer and raised it. Smash went the moon god, the sun god, and Ishtar, goddess of the morning star. Smash went Baal, the blessed golden calf. Smash went all the idols except for one into whose hands he placed the hammer.

When his father returned, he demanded to know what had happened.

"You must ask him," said Abraham, taunting his father and pointing to the single remaining statue.

King Nimrod grew furious when he heard what Abraham had done, and condemned Abraham to burn in a fire on the citadel of the city. But Abraham's God was watching. As the fire began to burn, God blew the wood and fire and Abraham over the cliff. Fire turned to water, wood turned to fishes, and Abraham emerged baptized in God's holy breath.

"It's interesting how the local Christians still honor Atargatis through their worship of the fishtailed Virgin Mary," I say, as we walk along the promenade where roses bloom in shades of orange and red and yellow.

Near the teal-green pools, we purchase bags of fish food at a kiosk.

"The fish in these pools are descendants of the sacred fish God created from pieces wood," says our friend Abraham.

At the edge of the one of the pools, sleek, greedy carp swarm to catch pellets we toss into the water, whipping the surface into white foam.

"We'd like to see the cave where Prophet Abraham's mother hid him from the pagan King Nimrod," we say to Abraham, who smiles and walks us across the honey-colored courtyard toward a covered arcade and the entrance to the Mevlid-i-Halil Camii, the Mosque of the Beloved, as the faithful call the prophet.

Water taps line a wall built into the mountain, where men in robes and women in gauzy headscarves perform their ablutions. We join them, relishing the sensuous, cool water as it slides over our skin, giving blessed respite from the sweltering heat.

At the women's entrance to the cave, preserved behind glass is an impression of the prophet's foot, with a curved insole and oversized toes. By our conservative calculations, the foot, double the size of a foot belonging to a mere mortal, would belong to a man at least twelve feet tall.

We've seen another oversized impression of a foot at the Topkapı Palace in Istanbul, an impression of the Prophet Mohammad's foot. It seems that Abraham and Mohammad literally towered over any competing prophets of their respective days. And I can't help thinking that in a land where mermaids swam in rivers and mariners and traders believed in moon gods, a prophet needed to be larger than life if he were establishing a new faith.

Angie has already entered the cave. I hunch my shoulders and follow her through a short tunnel into a crowded, dank cavern covered with carpets. We kneel on the floor, facing a Plexiglas-covered rock wall. But the altar, where believers say the child Abraham rested his head, is located on the opposite side of the cave wall.

"In the men's quarter," says Angie.

"*Sessiz noş*, shush," hisses an old woman kneeling beside us.

"At least we get the foot," I muse to a few more shushes.

Angie smiles and whispers, "And the boot, too."

A second group of women in flowered shalwar trousers enters the cave, eyeing us with a mixture of curiosity and suspicion. Jostling for space, they settle on their prayer rugs facing the rock wall.

When in Urfa, we decide, we'll do as the women do and bow our heads to pray. The cadence of women's voices as they chant words from the Qur'an mingles with the odor of unguents and sweat. Prayers rise and descend, echoing from the walls. "Allahu Akbar," chant the women, holding their arms up toward the wall. "God is great."

We're suddenly aware of our Western looks and manners, of the English language clattering in our heads in a space the women consider to be sacred and holy.

"I can't breathe," I say.

"Neither can I," says Angie. "I'm suffocating."

Bowing to the unadorned rock wall, Angie and I take our leave by imitating our companions. On hands and knees, we crawl backward toward the exit.

"I am sorry. I didn't know," Abraham says when we tell him that Abraham's altar is visible only from the men's section.

"But we saw Abraham's footprint," I say, feeding the last of the pellets to the fish.

"Fire into water, wood into fish, and a mermaid goddess waiting beneath the waves," says Angie. "Here, anything is possible."

The following day, we arrive at the local tourist office intent on hiring a guide to bring us to Harran, considered the oldest continually inhabited city in the world, and where Abraham and his wife Sarah briefly lived before settling in Canaan, the land of milk and honey.

The proprietor, who speaks no English, gestures to his assistant, who disappears down an alleyway. Minutes later, the assistant returns with a scrawny twelve-year-old boy possessing large brown eyes beneath a thatch of shiny black hair and a perfect row of white, oversized teeth that gleam when he smiles.

"I am Pasha," he says, acting every bit like the lord of his kingdom. "For one hundred fifty dollars U.S., I will be your guide."

Stunned by his impudence and the price of a day tour, we hesitate.

But in the course of negotiations, the tour company owner informs us that there are no other available guides, so we had better take the deal.

Caught in the bind of no supply and our great demand, we agree to the price and get into a late-model van with Pasha and the driver, a fatherly man with kind eyes.

The van heads south through waves of heat into a landscape punctuated by dusty-brown fields where longhair goats graze on piles of refuse. In lush, newly irrigated cotton fields, red-tinged buds burst open to reveal airy fluffs against green foliage.

At a checkpoint, the driver slows the van. Pasha waves gleefully to the guard, who smiles back, letting us pass through. Even with air-conditioning, sweat trickles into the hollows of our backs.

Harran rises from the plain as if mud has formed itself into twenty-foot-tall beehive shapes. Now, treeless and arid, with the sky as its focal point, Harran was known as the center of one of the world's oldest deities, Sin, the moon god, whose symbols, the crescent and star, now grace the Turkish flag.

For the Harranian priests and priestesses charting the movement of stars and planets, the story of the cosmos began with an unseen, supreme power called Marilaha and a trinity—Sin, the moon god, or bull of Heaven; Nikal, his wife; and their beautiful daughter, Ishtar, the morning star.

A myth associated with the powerful and sensual Sin went like this: If a girl went into the moonlight alone, she had to be careful, for if Sin gazed upon her, he might seduce her and make her pregnant.

"A convenient myth," says Angie. "But it may have saved many young women from being stoned to death."

Perhaps, we muse, the belief was a way to explain a pregnancy resulting from premarital sex or rape, one in which a girl might be spared a lifetime of shame or, worse, death by public stoning, and the man could remain nameless.

The moon god was worshipped as "the all-powerful one" into the eleventh century, when Harran fell to the Abbasid rulers of Arabia and Islam became the official religion. We've been told that in nearby villages, the locals still make secret offerings not only to Sin, but also to Atargatis, the fishtailed goddess.

The driver parks the van at a small visitors center made of mud bricks, where a boy sits on a plastic lawn chair next to a dusty display of postcards and drinks a Coke. Pasha leaps from the passenger seat and races ahead between the houses.

"Look, ladies," he cries from the top of a broken arched gate. "I'm king of the mountain!"

"You are indeed," I shout. Watching his carefree exuberance, I find myself missing my daughter, Sarah, with her own curiosity and playfulness.

Pasha lifts his arms above his head in triumph, and Angie snaps his picture.

Before we reach him, he's already scampered into the rubble of the world's oldest university. In the eleventh century, when Europe was in its Dark Ages, Harran University became a center of Islamic scholarship. Academic studies included theology, astronomy, medicine, mathematics, philosophy, and translations of works by Plato, Aristotle, and Plotinus into Arabic and Persian.

"This way, ladies. Follow me!" yells Pasha.

He climbs over mounds of potsherds and picks up a few terracotta pieces about six inches across, once part of a large amphora, and hands them to us. I trace the ribbed edges with my fingertips and imagine a young woman standing by a well at dusk, a thin cotton veil covering her hair. She fills her water jug and carries the heavy vessel on her shoulder, hurrying home before the moon, intent on seducing her, rises in the sky.

"You can keep those pieces of clay," says Pasha. "They are my presents to you."

I look at Angie, tempted to put the potsherd in my pocket.

"No, we can't," she says reluctantly. "An archaeologist might miss them."

"An archaeologist won't miss them at all," Pasha says, and stops. His face grows serious. He scratches his head. "There are so many pots to choose from and all of them so very old, ladies. So old it makes my head hurt."

In what might be our most expensive tour yet, we can't help but laugh at the exuberance of our adolescent guide. And he's right: Trying to untangle all this history could give anyone a headache.

Back in the van, Pasha explains that if we had more time, he could take us to the caves of the Sabians, heirs of Sin, who worshipped the sun, moon, and stars, but we must be back in Urfa before the afternoon curfew closes the road.

"Please, you may ask anything," says Pasha, settling into the passenger seat and yawning. He slides an arm over the center console, rests his head on his bicep and closes his eyes. The driver gently brushes unruly bangs from Pasha's face.

On our way back to our hotel, we stop at the archaeological museum. There are statues of goddesses with full, rounded breasts and bellies and a totem of the mermaid Atargatis with a womb carved into her belly.

There are statues of Sin with a lapis-lazuli beard, the color of the night sky, flowing to his waist, with the horns of a bull adorning his crown. Every evening after sunset, he embarks on his ship, the crescent moon, and navigates the night sky. And every month, the ship transforms into a shining orb, showing Sin's full power. And when the ship disappears and Sin hides his face under the cover of darkness, the gods consult him, calling him the wise man in the moon.

The following morning, Abraham asks his friend, a taxi driver named Başir, to bring us to the caves of Sin.

Başir, a stout fellow with a mullet haircut, dressed in a shiny blue tracksuit, hugs us a little too boldly before ushering us to his waiting taxi.

"I will bring you to a very secret place where only the villagers know the caves," he says, settling Angie into the front seat and me into the back. He pulls out an album from the glove compartment and hands it to Angie. Inside are twenty years' worth of photographs and business cards, all from tourists Başir guided into the nether regions of Mesopotamia.

"Later, when we have our picnic, we will take a photograph together," he says. "You will send it to me and I will put it in my album."

He pats Angie's knee with a little more familiarity than is necessary and hands her a business card. Her face freezes, and she moves as close to the passenger side of the car as she can.

At first, it seems we've found Dürzü's spiritual cousin. But Başir, a middle-age flirt, is equally eager to share information about how much he loves his four children and his wife, how his wife not only takes care of the children but also works part time in a dentist's office.

"I would love to meet her," I say.

"Maybe next time," he says, pulling the car to a roadside stand where hand gestures and a loud discussion result in the purchase of a watermelon, a cucumber, and a tomato.

"For our picnic," he says, setting the watermelon on the back seat next to me.

He breezes through the same checkpoint we passed with Pasha the day before. Soon the taxi leaves the main road, following a dirt track through a village where metal beds line the rooftops, waiting for the evening coolness to return. A boy on horseback kicks up a cloud of dust in an effort to race beside the taxi, but Başir presses the gas pedal, leaving the boy to become a mirage shimmering in sun-scattered dust.

The sky has turned white in the heat. I cough and drape my cotton scarf over my face, protecting my nose and mouth from dust.

I think of one of Angie's and my role models, the late nineteenth- and early twentieth-century British explorer Gertrude Bell, who traversed these dusty roads, mapping locations of Syrian Orthodox monasteries and churches. Later, she became a mentor to a young T. E. Lawrence, the soon-to-be-famous Lawrence of Arabia, sharing with him the customs of the region's tribes before settling in Baghdad, where she created the National Museum of Iraq.

Despite the heat, we imagine Lawrence, in flowing white robes, and Bell, wearing her trademark broad-brimmed hat and khaki skirt, taking a break for afternoon tea, Earl Grey in Wedgwood cups Bell has brought from England.

A hamlet of mud houses rises from the haze. Başir pulls to a stop. Three men in white caftans approach the car, their red and white pat- terned *kaffiyehs* held in place with black headbands.

Başir greets the men with kisses on each cheek and a hearty round of greetings before introducing us to Selim, the tribal leader.

Tall and elegant, Selim barely nods before turning his back to us and speaking in Arabic to Başir. While the men bond over cigarettes and an elaborate lighting ritual involving the passing of a single ciga- rette to light the rest, Angie and I gravitate toward a group of women and children who have emerged from a small, rectangular-shaped mud house with a satellite dish on its roof.

We form our own tribe, admiring one another's clothes, hair, and jewelry. The women wear engraved silver cuffs at their wrists and strands of lapis beads at their ankles. I notice they have blue tattoos below their lips, similar to those of the woman we saw in the bazaar.

Angie has brought a Polaroid camera and interrupts Başir to ask if she can take photos of the women, which she will give to them as gifts.

Başir gestures and speaks to Selim. The women look at their hus- band and hurry back into their house.

"I hope I didn't offend them," says Angie.

"Not at all," Başir smiles broadly. "The women are very pleased and are changing into their wedding clothes."

After we've taken photos of the men, the women return wearing patchwork skirts, white blouses, and beaded metal belts that proclaim their married status. A woman in a skirt sewn from shiny green squares of fabric and an orange-flowered, velvet vest over a dirty white blouse holds her red-haired, ringlet-curled baby toward us. A fly buzzes around his snot-crusted nose. He doesn't seem to mind as he intently watches Angie snap pictures.

The women smell of dust, sweat, and sour milk as they huddle around us and watch the images come into focus. The baby looks at a photo of himself and his mother. His mouth creases into a smile, and the air fills with his giggles.

"Selim will show you the caves now," Başir interrupts in a clipped tone that indicates we've spent enough time with the women.

With a single glance from Selim, his wives and their children dart back to the house and out of sight, leaving us in a strange netherworld where we've become neither male nor female, where we might as well be aliens.

The men won't look at us and speak through Başir as we follow them toward mounds of earth rising in a gentle undulation of landscape enveloped in dirt and sand. A boy motions us through the dark entrance of the first cave, but the stench of urine and feces drives us back. We aren't sure whether he was giving us the opportunity to use the facilities or whether the town toilet also houses mysterious secrets of the cult of Sin.

"*Henah*, here!" he says and leads us into the second cave.

Our eyes slowly adjust to the smoke-gray light. Shadowy, life-size carvings of planetary gods and priests appear on the curved walls, carrying scepters and wearing robes and tall, conical hats. At the farthest recess of the cave stands a six-foot-tall Sin, his face gouged by vandals, his garments chiseled away.

Above Sin's head hovers the crescent moon, cradling the morning star. Inscriptions written in a Syrian Aramaic, which none of the men can read, share wall space with the bas-relief figures.

"I feel an intense strange energy in this cave," says Angie.

I feel energy, too, radiating from the cave's ancient walls. Başir says that this was one of several caves used for rituals. We can almost see women and men bearing small offerings and praying for sick children, a happy marriage, to be a better friend and neighbor.

When we emerge into sunlight, we wonder at the likelihood of anyone preserving these caves in the middle of the Mesopotamian desert. Furthermore, we wonder, how many unexplored places like this exist?

I imagine a new Bible Studies curriculum where every child would be required to see this land of traders and faiths in order to grasp how complicated it must have been to worship so many gods and goddesses; how, over time, as astronomers charted the skies, people began to realize that there was something beyond the moon and stars. How religion evolves and much of what we take to be facts are stories.

Although curfew approaches, Başir insists that we stop for what he considers the highlight of our day, the picnic.

The car speeds past monotonous scenery until he finds a dirt track off the highway, which dead-ends near a stand of small trees and brush surrounding a clearing.

From the car we retrieve water, cheese and olives wrapped in butcher-block paper, the watermelon, tomato, and cucumber. Başir spreads out a blanket and we arrange the feast. After deftly peeling the tomato, he slices it in the palm of his hand and repeats the procedure with the cucumber.

Last but not least, he produces a small bottle of rakı. "To lift our spirits," he says.

Angie snaps Polaroid photos for Başir's album. Cicadas chirr a late-afternoon song. A warm breeze coaxes sweetness from the grasses. On the highway, three army tanks rumble toward Urfa.

"It must be near curfew," says Angie.

"Drink up," says Başir, checking his watch and pouring an extra splash of rakı into his cup.

The last tank slows as it passes, than comes to a halt. A soldier in the turret carefully scouts the field. We might have blended in except for my hot pink T-shirt and Başir's yellow taxi.

"Allah, Allah," mutters Başir when four soldiers get out, AK-47s in hand.

Three soldiers walk toward us. Two take up positions in the grass, their guns pointing to the hillside. The third walks over to Başir. Angie nudges me to look at the fourth soldier, who stops short and stands behind a large bush. His rifle site levels in our direction.

My back twitches, anticipating the sting of a bullet. Blood beats in my eardrums, but I sit perfectly still, trying to concentrate on the song of the cicadas.

The soldier speaks to Başir, who asks us to show our passports.

"He says I should know better than to bring you here," Başir adds as we hand over the passports.

One of the soldiers looks at the pictures spread across the blanket and asks about them.

"I told him they are just tourist photographs and that you are not spies," says Başir.

"Maybe they would like a picture for their mothers," says Angie, her voice much calmer than I feel.

Başir makes the offer, turning on the charm we've seen him display all afternoon.

The three soldiers slightly loosen their grips on the rifles.

"I told them they could send the photos to their girlfriends, not their mothers," whispers Başir.

Whatever fear Angie might feel, I see none of it in her actions as the soldiers take turns posing for their portraits, straightening their backs and positioning their rifles across their chests, then waving the photos in an effort to rush the development process.

The fourth soldier pushes through the brush.

"*Hayir*, no. You must pack up now and leave," the soldier says in English.

His words motivate us into action. We gather the leftover food and our backpacks. The senior officer holds the passenger car door open and speaks to Başir.

Then he turns to us. "We will escort you back to Urfa," he says politely.

And sure enough, we reach Urfa just after curfew, followed by a camouflage-colored tank, its gun pointed toward the horizon.

Chapter Twelve

THE EDUCATION OF MUSTAFA

Two tightrope walkers cannot perform on the same tightrope.
—Turkish proverb

Angie

With a tasseled black loafer, hotel manager Muharrem holds open the elevator door and gives us a curious glance before adjusting his maroon and gray striped tie. "Ah," he says, noticing our damp hair. "You have visited our hamam. Did you find it relaxing?"

"It was fine," I say, ignoring Joy's pointed gaze and noticing instead the flecks of pale gold in Muharrem's hazel eyes.

What I don't add is that when we arrived at the Mardin bus station, our cab driver had insisted on dropping us off at this large, expensive hotel outside the city limits. Too tired to argue, Joy and I had agreed to pull out our credit cards and enjoy the hotel's amenities.

Or that when we took advantage of one of those amenities, a "full service" hamam, the only attendant was male, and we were his only guests, which made us uncomfortable.

No sooner had we stretched out on the warm, marble belly stone and closed our eyes than we heard a knock on the steam-bath door. "Soap, shampoo?" the attendant called, cracking the door open, at which point we gathered our towels and left.

The attendant may have been sincere in his offer, but we had wanted to be left alone.

In a few days, we are to meet with KAMER, an organization based in Diyarbakır that provides counseling and shelter for women who are targets of *recem*, honor killings. Recem, practiced as part of tribal law, particularly in Kurdish communities, says that a woman who has had sex with a man other than her husband, even when she is raped, dishonors her family and must be killed by a brother, father, or another family member. Often the man with whom she had sex is killed, too, so the score between families remains even.

We first learned of KAMER from our friend and guide Simla in Istanbul years earlier, when discussing women's rights. Back in the States, I read an article in the *New York Times* about a young, unmarried, pregnant woman from a small village in the region who died after her family members crushed her skull by stoning. KAMER's staff and volunteers cared for the woman, who lingered for months before she died of her injuries. We wanted to know more about these courageous women.

"You must join me for a drink in the lounge," insists Muharrem.

When we left the hamam, Joy had warned me not to talk to anyone. "Don't even make eye contact," she said.

She checks her watch. It's already ten o'clock. She's been reading Orhan Pamuk's novel *The New Life*, and I can see that all she wants is to settle in bed with her book. But Muharrem looks so hopeful.

Her face softens. "Just one drink," she says, looking at me.

"OK," I say, accepting his invitation. "Give us a few minutes to change."

"Oh, but the singer doesn't go on stage until midnight," he smiles, cutting me off. "Take your time. I'll meet you at eleven thirty."

The door closes and the elevator starts its way up to our fourth floor room.

"Too late to back out now," I say. "He *is* cute, don't you think?"

"OK, then *you* go," retorts Joy.

In the end, she agrees to join me, pulling on jeans and a flowered blouse that gives off a puff of dust when she lifts it from her suitcase.

"We can't get into *that* much trouble if there are two of us," I say to my unamused travel partner.

Muharrem rises from a table next to a wide dance floor and pulls out chairs. Although the lounge can easily accommodate a few hundred people, the only other guests are four Turkish businessmen in suits and ties sitting at a table near the stage, immersed in an animated discussion over highballs. With a snap of his fingers, Muharrem orders a round of rakı, a plate of melon slices laced with pomegranate seeds, and glasses of a clear red beverage called *şalgam*, a concoction of purple carrots and turnips fermented with bulgur. It's a traditional tonic in southeastern Turkey, "To prevent a hangover," Muharrem says.

We nurse our drinks. Precisely at midnight a strobe light flashes through the lounge, announcing the arrival of a three-piece band and the singer, a petite brunette from Istanbul dressed in a leopard-skin print minidress and four-inch platform heels.

The band launches into a pop tune featuring an oud and a drum. Muharrem presses palm to heart and with calculated charm invites Joy to dance. I'm betting that once she gets on the dance floor, she'll rally back to life. The singer, thrilled to have an audience, shimmies her hips as Joy and Muharrem clap in time to the beat.

The next song, a sultry ballad, has been reserved for me. With his hand firmly pressed against my back, Muharrem leads me to the dance floor and pulls me close, looking directly into my eyes as if no one else is in the room.

"I am so very happy to see Americans in Mardin," he says, lightly pressing his cheek to mine. "The last hotel I managed was in Ankara, where I had many friends from the American embassy, but few single women like you." He takes a step back and gazes into my eyes.

All symptoms of fatigue subside. I feel feminine and sexy in his arms.

One of the businessmen removes his tie and opens the top two buttons of his gray striped shirt to reveal black chest hair sprouting beneath the collar of a crisp cotton undershirt. He walks over to Joy and invites her out to the floor for the next few numbers.

Muharrem and I join them, snapping our fingers and rolling hips and shoulders. The chanteuse shakes her waist-length hair and moves from the stage to the dance floor, tossing handfuls of cocktail napkins over us.

"This is a tradition to express pleasure at our dancing skills," says Muharrem, brushing napkins from my forehead.

When the music stops at four a.m., Muharrem escorts us back to our room, giving me a disappointed smile when I bid him goodnight.

"Perhaps I will see you tomorrow night?" he whispers, brushing my cheek with a kiss as I close the door.

"That was fun," I say the following morning after a second cup of coffee.

Joy smiles at the irony of dancing the night away, ankle-deep in cocktail napkins, while our friends and families worry about our safety.

"So, what about Muharrem?" she says.

"I don't know," I say. "Maybe I'll see him tonight."

Later, in the lobby, he waves us over to the front desk, where he is sorting through reservations.

"Canım," he says to me. "I have been waiting for you. I am deeply sorry, but I must be in Ankara for a meeting. Please, if you need anything, call my cell phone." He hands me his business card.

Eager to confirm our meeting with KAMER, Joy asks him if he could make a phone call to their office on our behalf.

"You may want an interpreter," Muharrem says when he hangs up the phone. "I'm not sure how much English they speak. I must go now or I will be late, but thank you for last night." He takes my right hand and brushes the tips of my fingers with his lips.

"Just as well," Joy says when I admit my disappointment. "Otherwise I might have lost my travel partner."

"It *was* getting pretty steamy," I tease.

Mardin's cream-colored limestone houses wind up and around the hillside like rows of pearls threaded along an elegant strand. White lace curtains and flower boxes filled with scarlet geraniums adorn windows overlooking the rooftops of the houses below. After climbing the steep stairs carved into the cliff that leads to town, we stop to catch our breath. Squares of earth in muted hues of brown and green drift toward Syria like crumpled newsprint left out too long under the blazing sun. On the edge of the Mesopotamian plain, our hotel rises from a dirt hillock like a giant box store.

On busy Birinci Caddesi, Mardin's main hub, eighteen-karat gold bracelets, chain necklaces, and pendants shimmer beneath the display-case lights of jewelry shops. They are destined to be gifts for Muslim and Christian brides alike, since Mardin's population has long been a mix of both religions.

"Let's have a look," says Joy, pointing to a gold chain-mail bracelet inlaid with circles of smooth, flawless Egyptian turquoise.

She slips into the shop before I can stop her.

"Please take a seat," says a cherub-faced young man with close-cropped hair, wearing a red knit polo shirt. Focused on a small scale holding silver chains, he doesn't look up but continues to punch numbers into a calculator.

"I was looking at a bracelet," says Joy.

"Yes, this one, I think," he says, setting down his calculator and plucking the gold bracelet from the window case. He reaches across the desk and fastens the bracelet around Joy's wrist. A small chain dangling from the clasp holds a gold openwork square embedded with turquoise in the shape of a cross.

He smiles as if he's never seen anything so beautiful.

"Are you German, British, Australian?" he asks, chiding himself when Joy mentions she's from New Jersey.

"Ah," he says, turning to slide a CD into his player. "There used to be many American soldiers stationed at the NATO base, but not so many since the wars in Afghanistan and Iraq." He adds, "I've never been to the States, but a few of my American friends were from Fort Dix in New Jersey. That's how I know Tom Waits and Bruce Springsteen."

From two small speakers mounted on the back wall, Tom Waits's throaty "Jersey Girl" fills the room. "I'm in love with a Jersey girl," the young man coos to Joy.

By the time glasses of tea arrive, we've learned his name, Gabriel, and that he's a Syrian Orthodox Christian who runs the jewelry business, which has been in his family for several generations. He lives with his father, grandmother, and sisters in a compound at least five hundred years old and has a passion for world music, movies, and Angelina Jolie.

"Many Christians were expelled before the republic was formed," he says, gazing at a woman in a yellow headscarf examining the jewelry in the window. "But this *is* a land of Christians. We've been here since the first church was founded in a cave in Antakya. We aren't going anywhere. Besides," he laughs, "who would run the jewelry shops?"

He goes on to say that Muslims and Christians have lived together in Mardin for more than a thousand years. "And I have many Muslim friends," he adds.

But when the noon prayer blasts from a nearby mosque, the conversation stops. He arches his thin eyebrows and asks Joy to close the door.

"Why do they need loudspeakers?" he says. "Our church bells ring only once a week, not five times a day."

He changes the CD and turns up the volume, replacing Tom Waits with the sultry voice of French singer Jane Birkin.

Glancing back at his calculator, he tells Joy, "Please, wear the bracelet. If you choose to keep it, you can pay me later. And please, come back at five. I will take you to meet my grandmother. She is an artist and paints pictures of saints on cloth.

"And, Angie, don't worry," he assures me. "I can get another bracelet for you."

With matching bracelets on our wrists, we follow Gabriel uphill past his shop.

He opens a thick wooden door to a courtyard where a goat tethered to an iron bed frame munches on weeds. "Our family has lived here for at least seven generations. This was probably a cave and my ancestors were Neanderthals," he jokes.

In the living room, family portraits of weddings and men in military uniforms vie for wall space with a print of Leonardo da Vinci's *The Last Supper*, crosses, icons of the Virgin Mary, and a Technicolor print of Jesus with hologram eyes that wink at us when we pass.

He ushers us into a studio, where white cotton cloths painted with almond-eyed saints hang from ceiling to floor. His grandmother sits at a long table behind jars of brushes and paints. Her fingers, stained with black dye, hold a wooden stamp carved with leaves and scrolls. In a blue-and-white-checked dress covered by a white bib apron, and with silver hair plaited and wound around the crown of her head, she reminds me of my Dutch grandmother, a farmer's wife who raised seven children. When she looks up from a piece of fabric held close to her face, she reveals eyes that appear to be twice their actual size thanks to bottle-thick glasses. Those eyes hold the same tenacious quality I saw in my grandmother's eyes.

She instructs Gabriel to show us her work, and he dutifully pulls several cloths from those stacked on tables and chairs. "Many of her paintings hang in our church," he says.

The rustic, religious folk-art designs have little appeal to us, except for one, a mermaid saint with large eyes, long, yellow, flowing hair; and a green-scaled tail, its fin flipped upward.

"Atargatis," says Joy, looking at me.

"She is just a symbol we have always seen, and one that my grandmother likes to paint. I think the mermaid must be from your Disneyland," Gabriel says with a chuckle.

"Not exactly," says Joy, who goes on to share what we've learned about the goddess of rivers and streams. "You see, she never left."

"Maybe this is true," says Gabriel.

Before he walks us back to our hotel, he opens a trap door under a carpet in the hallway to show us the family's wine cellar. A ladder leads him down into a large hole carved beneath the floor. He opens a stone vat, dips a ladle into last year's harvest, pours smoky-sweet wine into three tulip-shaped glasses, and offers a toast to our new friendship, our families, the lady of the rivers, Mary and her son Jesus, and many more visits to his home.

Outside the Mardin post office, I pull my well-worn map from my backpack to measure the distance from Mardin to the town of Nusaybin, on the Syrian border. Thousands of Armenian, Greek, and Syrian Christians were deported to Syria through Nusaybin during World War I.

A young man dressed in a creased khaki-green suit, white dress shirt, and thin gold tie passes by with a dozen middle-school students in tow and turns around.

"Hello," he says. "I saw you yesterday in the jewelry shop on Birinci Caddesi." He glances at our map. "May I be of help? Where are you going?

"Nusaybin," says Joy, "if we can figure out how to get there."

He pushes wire-rimmed glasses up the bridge of his small nose.

"That would be here." He points to a black dot along a cross-hatched line, which represents a railroad, about an inch and a half south of Mardin.

"Please, I am Mustafa." He extends his right hand to us. "I am an English teacher, and these are my students."

"Hello, how are you?" asks a redheaded boy standing behind Mustafa. "Where . . . you . . . from?"

"Where *are* you from," corrects Mustafa, and the boy carefully repeats his question.

"America," we answer.

"Meeky Mouse," says the boy, and shyly holds out his wrist to show us a watch featuring Mickey Mouse, with arms that act as hour and minute hands.

Mustafa checks his own watch and looks at us as if he has an agenda in mind.

"I must get the children back to school," he says, scribbling his phone number on the edge of our map. "But I have a car; it would be an honor to drive you to Nusaybin. And," he adds, "it would be a wonderful opportunity to practice my English."

He notices our hesitation.

"Oh, I promise it would not be a problem. I would like to be of service to you during your visit in Mardin and can arrange to have another teacher take my afternoon classes."

Later, on our way back to the hotel, two boys heading home from school stop to ask our names and where we're from.

"How do you like the people of Mardin? Are they friendly?" asks one of the young Mardin diplomats.

"Oh, Mardin has the friendliest people in all of Turkey," I say.

"Especially the children," adds Joy, and they scamper off with broad smiles on their faces.

Mustafa arrives in front of our hotel in a midnight-blue, four-door Renault. An attractive, dark-haired woman wearing black jeans and a tailored, red blouse sits beside him. She eagerly emerges from the car to embrace us and share cheek kisses.

"I hope you don't mind," says Mustafa, opening the door to the back seat. "This is my colleague Aylin. I thought you might enjoy talking with her, too."

"Thank you," she says, her voice almost desperate. "I've only been in Mardin a few months and have seen nothing of the area, except the school, of course. Mustafa thought I'd like to meet you. I grew up in Antalya and went to university in Ankara. It is much more conservative here than what I'm used to."

"So when you graduated, the university exiled you to eastern Turkey," I say. "And you're going through culture shock."

Aylin laughs with relief. "You understand."

"There is much to show you," says Mustafa, keeping us on schedule. "First, we will see Kaşımpaşa Medresesi. It was built in the thirteenth century and was one of our region's great universities."

Like Gabriel eager for us to meet his grandmother, Mustafa wants to show us the best of Mardin's Muslim world.

At the Kaşımpaşa Medresesi's gate, Mustafa speaks to the caretaker, a middle-aged man in an argyle sweater vest and tweed golf cap, who brings us into the courtyard.

"This was a very famous school." He leads us into another courtyard where shafts of dusty sunlight stream through windows cut into stone. "Here, students learned about the planets and engaged in philosophical debates about how the world and the heavens worked. You see, an education was not only a quest for knowledge, but to make the world a better place in honor of Allah."

He leads us up a staircase to an expansive flat rooftop. Anatolia undulates to the north in green-gray hills and valleys, while the Mesopotamian plane rolls flat and hazy toward the southern horizon. We imagine bedrolls filling the rooftop on hot summer nights, stars shining above, and students with telescopes charting the movement of the heavens.

In the central courtyard below, a large rectangular pool reflects the blue sky. From an ornate font, springwater bubbles into a six-inch-wide canal that feeds the pool.

"The spring represents birth," says Mustafa. "The channel our life's journey, and the pool represents Heaven."

"What are those marks on the wall?" asks Joy.

We follow her gaze toward reddish-brown splotches on a wall opposite the pool.

"Come with me," says Mustafa, bringing us back down the staircase. He gives instructions to the caretaker, who fills a plastic bucket from the fountain and tosses water against the wall to enhance the stains.

"It is the blood of Kaşım Pasha," says Mustafa. "Kaşım's enemies murdered him in this very place. Because his sister was filled with grief, she took his bloody shirt and threw it against the wall for all to see how brutally he had been killed. No one has been able to wash his blood from the wall."

Aylin drops her gaze toward Mustafa. "Folk tales," she says, shaking her head, and soon they are having a serious discussion in Turkish.

Careful not to exclude us, Mustafa says that Aylin has brought up the subject of recem, honor killings, and has told him that we've shared with her our plans to meet with the women of KAMER in Diyarbakır.

"We hear stories about recem," he says. "But I think most of these things happened many years ago."

Aylin interrupts him, her voice rising. "It happens today, right here in southeastern Turkey."

She walks to the edge of the courtyard and gazes into the Mesopotamian haze.

"We're meeting with KAMER's founder, Nebahat Akkoç," I say.

Mustafa opens his palms in a gesture of resignation and looks at us.

Joy glances at me and says, "We *do* need a translator."

"Yes," I say. "Would you be willing to translate for us?"

"Of course," he says, regaining his composure and gazing toward Aylin.

"We still have time to visit Nusaybin," a relieved Mustafa says after we drop Aylin off at the school for her afternoon classes.

We take the E90 highway east and follow the Baghdad Railway toward Nusaybin, on the frontier at the Syrian border.

On a shoulder near the steel railroad tracks, Mustafa stops the car, and I roll down the window to take a photo of a half-dozen sheep grazing on weeds growing next to the rails.

One of the twentieth century's great engineering feats, construction of the Baghdad Railway began in 1903, when, at the request of the Ottoman Empire, German engineers embarked on a project to connect Berlin to Baghdad through Turkey, with the aim of gaining access to the Persian Gulf. More than one thousand workers carved roads into steep mountain peaks, built a series of bridges over gorges and rivers, and bored tunnels through the Taurus Mountains.

After many delays, including the collapse of the Ottoman Empire and the founding of the Turkish republic, the railway was completed in 1940. A new rail line, the Taurus Express, picked up where the Orient Express left off, bringing passengers from Istanbul through Nusaybin to Baghdad.

Men barely look up from vegetable carts and teahouses when we drive through Nusaybin. Nothing is left, it seems, from the days when Nusaybin was an important stop on the Baghdad Railway. The gardens of white roses that once gave Nusaybin the title "The Most Beautiful City in the World" have vanished.

Mustafa pulls into an empty dirt parking lot at the border, where two Greek columns stand in a field protected by a ten-foot-high fence with barbed-wire coils around its top. A bridge spans the Djada River, which separates Nusaybin from the Syrian city of Al-Qamishli.

"I have relatives just across the border," he says, and admits that he's never been to Syria, or to Nusaybin, for that matter. "I'll see if we can drive across."

Joy and I explain that neither of us has a visa. But Mustafa, confident in his diplomatic skills, tells us to wait in the car and approaches the soldier guarding the fence. When Mustafa takes off his sunglasses and slides a hand into his suit jacket pocket to pull out a pen, the soldier shouts and points his rifle at him.

Joy gasps audibly.

"*Dur! Dur!*" the soldier yells. "Stop! Stop!"

Unfazed, Mustafa continues talking to the guard and holds up a pen. "I'm going to the station to speak to the officer in charge," he calls.

Twenty minutes later, he returns.

"I am sorry, but I cannot get you into Syria," he says, and pulls out his pen. "You see, they didn't shoot me." With a wide grin, he twirls his pen through his fingertips. "Because the pen *is* mightier than the sword."

Early the next morning dressed in jeans, a checked shirt, and a multipocketed, photojournalist-style vest, Mustafa greets us in the hotel lobby and walks us to his car. A serious-looking young man waits in the passenger seat.

"This is my brother, Murat," says Mustafa. "He will keep me company on the drive back. But only if it is OK with you."

Murat, already settled in for the trip, nods his head at the mention of his name.

"Of course," Joy and I say in unison. We've grown fond of Mustafa and guess he may be uncomfortable at KAMER without an escort.

Once we're on the road, Murat admonishes Mustafa for missing morning prayers. His chiding surprises us until we learn that although Murat seems younger than Mustafa, he is the older brother and has the right to pull rank.

"Mustafa is not a good Muslim," says Murat.

To us, Mustafa seems devout. He doesn't smoke or drink alcohol, and he goes to the mosque every Friday.

"Once a week is enough for me," says Mustafa. "I must take after my great-grandmother," he adds, shrugging off Murat's taunts. "Did I tell you that she was a Syrian Orthodox Christian?"

Murat shakes his head as if Mustafa has just uttered a blasphemy.

"But it is true," says Mustafa. "Our grandmother's family left Mardin years ago."

Unfamiliar with the city of Diyarbakır, Mustafa circles the ten-foot-thick, black basalt walls of the city until he reaches the entrance to the Mardin Gate.

"It is almost time for the noon prayer," he says. "Murat wants to pray at the Ulu Camii, but I can stay here with you."

We've come prepared with headscarves and suggest that we all go to the mosque.

Murat washes his hands and face at a fountain outside the mosque and enters moments before the muezzin's call to prayer. Mustafa stays behind to help us locate the women's section, usually cordoned off by a curtain or screen to the side or back of the mosque. When he can't find it, he stops an old man who is entering the mosque wearing a traditional skullcap and baggy pants.

Turning back to us, Mustafa points across the courtyard to the large, dark building. "He says the women's section is in the medrese. But I don't think anyone is praying there."

He looks as baffled as we feel.

When he later explains the situation to his brother, Murat has a ready answer: "Women are already close to God and do not need to go to the mosque every day."

Perhaps they're too busy taking care of the children and cooking dinner for the husbands who are praying in the mosque, we think, but we decide to put aside the subject of women's rights until our interview at KAMER.

Arms folded across her chest, Nebahat Akkoç stands on the street-level patio of a four-story apartment building in a neighborhood of middle-class houses just outside the city walls. A blue, four-by-six-foot sign with KAMER in white letters distinguishes her organization from the other apartment buildings on the street.

We get out and introduce ourselves while Mustafa parallel parks the car in front. A cautious smile crosses Akkoç's lips when she sees Mustafa and Murat.

One by one, eight women lined up behind her step forward to shake our hands. A tall, thin woman with cropped auburn hair invites us to sit at a patio table set with a white linen tablecloth, crystal glasses, small plates, and an assortment of pastries.

Akkoç motions us to sit across from her.

Murat perches on a ledge at the edge of the patio while Mustafa settles between us so he can easily translate.

The women stoically shift their gazes to Mustafa and Murat.

Mustafa shows them his three-inch-thick Turkish-English dictionary and sets it on the table.

"Thank you for agreeing to meet with us," says Joy.

Akkoç nods politely as if to say, "Yes, sure, get on with it, and why did you bring these men with you?"

"Mustafa is our friend," adds Joy, hoping to clarify Akkoç's unasked question. "He has been good enough to drive us here and act as our translator."

"I am an English teacher from Mardin, and my brother teaches computer classes," Mustafa adds, hoping that his and Murat's educational backgrounds will garner points.

Akkoç, who is Kurdish, a former primary school teacher, and a mother of two, shares her story. In 1993, at the height of civil war between Kurdish separatists and the Turkish government, Akkoç's husband, a union activist, was murdered. Although it was never proved, Akkoç believes Turkish security officials gave the orders to have him killed.

Shortly after her husband's death, Akkoç was arrested, jailed, and tortured by the police. When she was released, she took her case to the European Court of Human Rights and was awarded 150,000 euros.

"I thought about torture and believed that only a child who had been exposed to violence in the home could inflict such pain on another," she says, through Mustafa's translation. "And I thought, to make a change for peace, we must educate women and their children. That is why I founded KAMER and opened this center in 1997."

A young woman from the KAMER restaurant serves water and sodas. Open to the public, the restaurant allows women the opportunity to earn money for themselves.

While drinks are poured, the women at the table discuss the *New York Times* article about Cemse Allak, who lived not far from Diyarbakır. Because she was unmarried and impregnated by a local man who may have raped her, Cemse's father and brother stoned her and left her for dead.

"First, her baby died," says Akkoç. "She died later in hospital."

Akkoç explains how the women at KAMER took turns bringing Cemse her medicine, bathing her, and pushing her into sunlight in a wheelchair.

"After Cemse died," she adds, "her family did not claim her body, so we arranged for the funeral."

"I was one of the people in the newspaper photograph," says a redheaded woman. She adds that Cemse was buried in a municipal cemetery. Led by the women of KAMER, who carried the coffin, nearly one hundred women attended the funeral. None was a member of Cemse's family.

The women listen intently as Mustafa, his face flushed, translates.

We take a moment to praise him.

He reluctantly translates the compliments. "I am telling them that these are your words, not mine," he says, modestly.

Akkoç's face lights up as it dawns on her, just as it has to us, that Mustafa's desire to learn about her world is genuine.

With this small passing of an olive branch, several women uncross their arms, and the meeting takes on a lighter tone.

"Please call me Nebahat," Akkoç says, reassuring Mustafa that she's glad he came to translate.

"When we work with cases of violence toward women, we make an effort not to judge the perpetrators," she says.

Murat listens intently as Mustafa, ever the diplomat, unemotionally parrots the conversation between the women and us. Everyone laughs when he mistakenly translates a comment to me in Turkish and to Nebahat in English.

"Please eat," says Nebahat, and she pushes the platter of pastries toward us. I take a few cookies and a cream-filled roll. A girl of about eighteen refills our water glasses.

"I helped carry the coffin," says a woman, speaking of Cemse.

"It is my job to visit the villages when we hear of the threat of recem, to see if we can help," says another woman. Dark spiked hair frames her serious face.

She says that before 2005, Turkish law did not consider rape within wedlock a crime, and if a rapist married his victim, he could not be convicted. Under pressure from the European Union and activists such as the women of KAMER, laws are now being changed and enforced.

There's little joy in such an occupation, I think, and it seems likely that many of these women have been victims of abuse, too.

"We are making a small difference," offers Nebahat. "Even a single death from recem is one too many."

She insists on giving us a tour of the building. In a colorful playroom, walls display children's drawings. Sequined and chiffon costumes hang on a rack in the corner, along with a stack of books and board games.

"The children create plays here," says Nebahat. "We do not segregate the boys and girls. You see," she adds, looking at Mustafa, "it is not enough to only educate women. We must also educate our sons and daughters."

Joy smiles and asks Nebahat what she considers to be her greatest accomplishment.

"This building," says Nebahat, opening her arms. "It is our present and our future."

Spring

2007

Chapter Thirteen

THE NYMPH WHO RAN AWAY

Why do you follow me?
Any moment I can be
Nothing but a laurel-tree.

—*Edna St. Vincent Millay,* Daphne

Joy

On a warm spring morning, a girl of sixteen takes a sunbath on a rock in a grove of laurel trees by a river. Her golden brown skin absorbs sunlight; her auburn hair flecked with red and tawny highlights falls to her waist.

A man hides in the bushes and watches. How beautiful and fresh you are, he thinks. How tempting.

He leaps from his hiding place. A twig snaps.

She looks up and runs, but it's too late.

After traveling to nearly all of Turkey's borders, we find ourselves in the breakfast room of the Grand Antakya Hotel, in Turkey's Hatay Province, overlooking Cumhuriyet Caddesi, Antakya's main boulevard.

Young women stroll by in tight jeans and knee-high platform boots. Men in blazers over faded jeans, some with flat fisherman caps and round, wire-rim glasses, chat and make points with thin cigarettes.

A few women pass by in dark, conservative coats and tightly knotted headscarves, but others wear suits and dresses and pretty floral scarves tied loosely beneath their chins.

"If not for the Mediterranean light," says Angie, spreading our well-worn map of Anatolia across the table, "we could trick ourselves into thinking we're in Istanbul."

I remind Angie how six years earlier, our friend Simla had encouraged us to visit Antakya and the Hatay Province.

We had been sitting in the Women's Library and Information Centre in Istanbul's Fener neighborhood, sipping Turkish coffee and talking about women's issues, when Simla told us about recem in the southeast, a conversation that ultimately led us to Diyarbakır.

But we also spoke of the demise of the mother goddess and the rise of patriarchal religions, and said we were curious to visit Antakya because we knew the city as Antioch, home of the first Christian church.

"Of course you must go the Grotto of Saint Peter," Simla had said. "But there's more to see than just the church. In the ancient world, Antioch was an important city on the east-west trade routes, as important as Alexandria and Constantinople. Just outside the city of Antakya is a place called Harbiye, known in the ancient world as Daphne, where the Romans built exquisite villas in the laurel groves."

Now, as we study the map of Turkey, we see how Antakya, halfway between Jerusalem and Istanbul, doesn't quite fit inside Anatolia.

Our waitress, a friendly young woman in black pants and a starched white blouse, brings coffee to our table and smiles with curiosity when she sees our travel routes marked across the map.

Shaped like a bull, Anatolia leaps from the eastern edge of the Mediterranean basin toward North Africa and Europe. Its head juts into the Aegean and Mediterranean seas, almost touching the Greek Dodecanese Islands. Its back rises along the Black Sea, while its hindquarters push toward Asia.

The waitress presses her index finger against the map and outlines the Hatay Province. Lost to French Syria after the breakup of the Ottoman Empire and annexed by Turkey just before World War II, Hatay borders Syria to the east and juts south toward Lebanon along the Mediterranean Sea.

"We call Hatay the *erkeklik organı*," she says, blushing.

At first we don't understand.

"It gives the man his power," she says, the apples of her cheeks turning crimson as she again traces the elongated shape of the province.

"Oh," I say, looking at Angie, who lifts her eyebrows and flashes a knowing smile.

"The most important province in *all* of Turkey," says the waitress, laughing.

"Have you been to Harbiye, the grove of the nymph Daphne?" asks Angie, moving the conversation away from the subject of geographic anatomy.

"Evet, yes," says the girl. "It is a special place for family picnics and for couples, too. Sometimes I go with my boyfriend for tea and to sit beneath the waterfalls."

She lowers her eyes as if she doesn't want to reveal too much about her amorous adventures among the laurel leaves and goes on to explain some of the Hatay specialties awaiting us on the buffet table: *kekik*, a salad made from thyme leaves and sprinkled with lemon and pomegranate syrup; olive oil with *za'atar*, a mix of thyme, oregano, and sesame seeds, to be spread over white cheese; pureed fava beans with red pepper; and rich, thick yogurt sprinkled with dried mint.

After breakfast, we cross the Orontes River toward the Cave-Church of Saint Peter, carved into Mount Starius. Beneath a sky rich as teal silk, a flock of sparrows swirl in unison, searching for insects. We pass through the old bazaar, a mass of cobbled alleys.

"Perhaps the apostles Paul and Barnabas wandered through these streets preaching the Good News and avoiding Roman soldiers ready to chase them away," I muse.

"They would have had a big audience," says Angie, as we join a crowd at an open-air bakery to watch a young man pour a thin stream of batter onto a heated revolving stone. The batter sets into amber strands of wheat to be made into künefe, a dessert layered with thick cream, pistachios, and sugar syrup.

On a side street, shops advertise modest floor-length coats, heads-carves, and underwear including lace thongs and bikinis. From the friendly proprietress of one shop, we buy deep pink and red Syrian silk scarves before she sends us down a side street leading to the Grotto of Saint Peter.

Off Kurtuluş Caddesi, a path rises to an outcrop where poppies, thyme, chamomile, and daisies sprout between tufts of grass. Antakya settles into a dusty, blue mirage, dissolving into the Antioch of my Sunday-school lessons, a cosmopolitan city of Greeks, Romans, Jews, and pagans who believed in gods and goddesses and prophets and messiahs.

"Ladies. Souvenirs!"

Three giggling boys and two girls in school uniforms clamber up the hillside.

One of the boys holds out a crumpled paper bag. "Bones. Very, very cheap," he says, revealing the tips of two large teeth breaking through his upper gums when he grins.

He reaches a dirty hand into the bag and pulls out a human jawbone.

"One dollar American," he says, extending the bag. "*Eski*, old."

"You can't sell those," says Angie, reaching for the bag in an attempt to confiscate what might be sacred human remains—although what she'll do with them, I have no idea.

"*Nerede*, where did you get these?" I ask.

"From there."

He points past Saint Peter's church. The jawbone in his hand accidentally tilts, and molars scatter to the ground.

His companions seize their opportunity to get in on the sale, grabbing at the teeth and offering them for "American dollars."

"Allah, Allah," cries the boy, giving us a wounded glance before pawing through the dirt to reclaim the precious teeth.

Feeling sympathy for the little grave robbers, I dig into my pocket and pull out Turkish coins, giving a few liras to each child.

The girls seem pleased, but the boys let out a collective moan at their sale gone sour. With defeat in their eyes, they scamper down the hill, nimble as billy goats.

When we reach the church, the gate is closed. In the guardhouse a man in his midthirties sits at a desk, monitoring the homework of a boy and girl, who write in notebooks.

The boy leaps up at our knock. "You are looking for a ticket?" he says in British-inflected English. He rummages through the desk for a ticket pad and switches to Turkish to speak to his father.

The girl touches her father's hand and adds a pleading voice to the chorus. Smiling briefly, the father gives his children a reprieve to show the church to the "Chreestians."

The boy and his sister lead the way to an entrance whose similarity to any church we've known ends with a stone facade built during the First Crusade in 1098 and framing an opening carved into a cliff.

Saints Peter and Paul, who lived in Antioch, were thought to have preached here, establishing what is known as the first Christian church.

On the chalky dirt floor of the damp, vaulted cave, our footprints blend with those of the children. Water drips from a rock near the altar, beating an ancient pulse into a shallow depression of earth.

We try to imagine men and women moving toward the heavy stone altar, but the space is cold and empty. There are no restored frescoes, no relics, and no adornments, only a plaque announcing that believers who visit the church will receive plenary indulgence, a pardon for past sins.

Originally, indulgence meant a favor such as the forgiveness of a tax debt or the lessening of a punishment for a crime. But the early Christian Church adopted the practice to encourage followers to remain devout. Pilgrims could earn their way to Heaven by making journeys to sacred shrines, especially those where miracles were said to have occurred. During the First Crusade, Pope Urban II used plenary indulgence with great success to regain Jerusalem and the Holy Land from the Muslims.

"*Deus vult*—God wills it," Urban II declared, promising riches and women to his soldiers. And if a soldier died on the battlefield, he would go directly to paradise, where those very same riches and women—and eternal happiness—awaited him.

The boy beckons us to the left side of the stone altar and down a small passageway.

"Tunnels," he says.

"Many tombs," says the girl, making me think of the little grave robbers.

The boy climbs in and motions us to follow. Curious where the tunnel will lead, I wedge my way in. But I'm larger than the world's first Christians, and the opening quickly becomes too narrow. The tunnel, we learn, was used as an escape route for the early Christians, similar to the underground tunnels in Cappadocia.

Choking on fine dust, I back out, sending runnels of dirt to the floor. We wait with the girl until her brother reappears, holding a handful of grass to prove he made it to the surface.

Before we leave, we kneel at the spring by the altar to rinse the dust from our hands. I think of the cave at Sümela in Trabzon, the caves of Sin, and the Cave of the Bear on the island of Crete, imagining a lineage of men and women rinsing hands and feet in the life-giving water and praying for a moment of grace.

In the courtyard, as our eyes adjust to late-afternoon sunlight, we hear the children's father call their names.

The boy looks up and with a sweep of his hand brushes back a swath of wild daisies to reveal a path that will take us back to Antakya.

"Güle, güle, go happily, happily," says his sister, circling my waist with an affectionate hug.

"I will show you where you must get the minibus to Harbiye," our waitress says the next morning. "You will love this place."

On a side street near the bazaar, several people with packages are already boarding the dusty gray van. The waitress gives the driver instructions about where to drop us off and waves good-bye.

A half hour later, the bus stops in the parking lot by a tourist restaurant. "Harbiye," calls the driver.

We alight with a young couple in their twenties who twine arms and set forth along a path at the edge of the lush gorge, where the road toward Syria slips over the mountain range like a golden sash. The valley undulates in terraces of cypress and fruit trees. Poppies brighten the fields like tongues of flame. A waterfall tumbles into a fan of streams carrying the clean, astringent scent of laurel.

In the once-wealthy suburb of Daphne, the Greeks built a splen-did marble temple for the sun god, Apollo, and the Romans por-trayed their gods and goddesses in exquisite mosaics. Here the first Olympic Games were held, and people traveled from throughout the

Mediterranean to watch the finest athletes. It is said that in 40 CE, Mark Antony picked Daphne as the perfect setting in which to marry his queen, Cleopatra.

In the green light of the intoxicatingly fragrant laurel grove, next to a tea garden where ducks float serenely in a small pond, we come upon a man in a tall black hat. He is sitting at a low table, reading the Qur'an and chanting.

Soon, we notice potato chip bags and cigarette butts floating along the bank. In the underbrush we see candy wrappers and a soiled disposable diaper. Plastic water bottles bob like bloated fish in a stream leading to the pond.

"How disgusting," I say, unaware that the tea vendor is standing behind us, ready to take our order.

"Aman," he says, his voice apologetic. "Is a big problem. Only a few years ago, we did not have all this trash. Yes, people threw their garbage. We all did this, but it was not plastic. In my village, goats eat plastic and it stays in their stomachs. Sometimes the goats die. Yes, it is terrible." He shakes his head. "I think the government must set rules and make fines. Really, it is the only way we will learn."

"When we were kids," I say, "we used to throw trash from our car windows. Our government set up litter laws. They even had a song." I look at Angie, who smiles. "'Please, please, don't be a litterbug, 'cause every litter bit hurts,'" I sing.

"Yes," he says, excusing himself to bring tea. "This is what must happen here, too. But I hope they will write a better song."

Later, he clears our glasses and shows us a path between car-size boulders speckled with yellow, orange, and green lichen.

"Please, enjoy yourselves" he says. "It is so very beautiful, do not look at the trash."

In the grove, away from the trash, we climb between the boulders and find laurel trees the color of elephant hide holding up tender branches. New growth, supple as fingers, supports pale green leaves and luminous red buds. In this wild forest of tangled trees and vines, we imagine a lithe and gifted huntress named Daphne bestowing the healing secrets of *Laurus nobilis*, the noble laurel tree, to her mortal brothers and sisters.

Angie and I climb the tree's broad trunk onto two thick branches and stretch along the warm, smooth bark. Sunlight filters onto our skin from between the leaves. I close my eyes and imagine Daphne sitting at the river's edge.

She hears the heavy snap of a branch and sees a man twice her size, Apollo, the sun god, with glowing skin and blazing, hard eyes, coming toward her.

Her belly cramps with fear. She knows him, and so she jumps up and runs through the forest.

Apollo draws closer.

"Leave me alone!" she cries.

The wind lifts her skirt. Brambles scratch her arms and legs, drawing garlands of blood.

"Father," she calls. "Help me!"

"The faster you run," shouts Apollo, "the more I want you."

"Father!" pleads the radiant virgin.

Her father, Peneus, god of the river, hears her call. He loves his beautiful daughter more than his own life, and so he rises from the riverbed.

"I will save you, my daughter," he shouts.

Blinded by lust and ego, Apollo grabs Daphne by the shoulders.

"Stop!" commands Peneus.

Suddenly, Daphne's feet sink into earth. Her bones crack. Pain radiates from her joints into her muscles. Her dress falls away as her skin hardens into bark. She lifts her arms. Leaves sprout from her fingertips.

"Good-bye, father," she whispers.

Peneus slips beneath the river as he says, "May you live forever, daughter, and may your grove remain sacred."

Furious, Apollo reaches toward her once-silky hair, smells the fresh scent of laurel oil, and knows he has made a mistake.

"I am a god," he weeps. "And you should have listened to me."

One by one, he plucks leaves from her branches, weaves them into a crown, and places it on his head. "Every king shall wear a wreath of laurel leaves in tribute to my Daphne," he says.

But Daphne no longer hears his voice. Her branches arch toward a cloud-flecked sky as dark roots reach toward the underworld.

I think of Nebahat and the women of KAMER, working to protect their sisters who are running for their lives from men with desires no different than those of Apollo. And how, through the education of girls and boys, they are creating a new model for the future, one that moves beyond ancient customs.

The trees rustle in the breeze, laughing it seems, a chorus rising from the earth.

Angie climbs higher. Laurel leaves, soft as skin, release their scent into the humid air.

"Let's write a new story," she says. "One in which Apollo enters this sacred space as Daphne's equal."

Yes, I think. A story for my daughter.

Fall

2009

Chapter Fourteen

RETURN TO THE LYCIAN SEA

*Journeys, like artists, are born and not made. A thousand
differing circumstances contribute to them, few of them willed
or determined by the will—whatever we may think.
They flower spontaneously out of the demands of our
natures—and the best of them lead us not only outwards
in space, but inwards as well. Travel can be one of the
most rewarding forms of introspection . . .*

—*Lawrence Durrell*, Bitter Lemons

Angie

Lamplight gleams against photographs scattered across the red and black, diamond-patterned carpet I bought near the KAMER offices in Diyarbakır, images sorted by year and pulled from labeled boxes to be scanned into my computer.

I withdraw a photograph from a box labeled KALKAN. In a turquoise print sundress and Converse sneakers, I am leaning against the railing of the Sun Pension balcony, framed by magenta bougainvillea blossoms. Holding a sun visor in my hand, I am smiling at Joy, who snaps the picture with her Canon Rebel, the red bandana she uses as a lens cover dangling from the camera's strap. We're on our way to meet Bekir for a hike into the mountains where caper bushes bloom on the hillside in billows of pink flowers, where Bekir will pick plump buds. Later he will serve the home-brined delicacy over grilled fish.

From another box I pull a photograph of Nebahat Akkoç. She stands in front of her staff on the porch of her building, her warm smile at odds with arms crossed firmly beneath her breasts. Yet in her expression and those of the eight women behind her, I see an inner strength and compassion, and hope for the more than 40,000 women they have educated about the causes and impact of domestic violence. In 2008, the Turkish government named Nebahat social entrepreneur of the year.

I add this photo to others in the stack to be scanned into my computer.

The reason for this exercise is not, as I told Joy, simply to purge my photograph boxes, which were gathering dust on the floor of my closet. In the grove of Daphne, in fragrant sunlight among laurel trees, I'd had a revelation. Like a conflicted lover in a long-distance romance whose future remains uncertain, I'd wondered if my relationship with Turkey had come to an end. There, myth and reality had merged, and I had asked myself: Do I need to continue the search?

Yet when I returned home, I felt something missing in the solitude of my safe, predictable life.

Joy had summed it up during one of our talks on the Sun Pension balcony. "I remember my first trip abroad," she had said. "Wendy and I got off our flight in Athens, and in the domestic terminal we picked the first plane leaving for the Greek islands. We arrived on the island of Kos at night, found a hotel, and in the morning awoke to a mauve and lavender sunrise over the Turkish coast. In that moment, the world expanded, and I found the path I'm still walking. '*E Zoe*,' as my Greek friends would say. Life in its grandest sense."

Yes, I think. *Yaşam* in Turkish—The Life.

These thoughts swirl through my mind as the stack of photos I've put aside to be copied grows.

Two days earlier, I had received an e-mail from our friend Kate, whom we first met in Kalkan. She had taken the expat plunge a few years earlier and left her career as a dental hygienist in San Francisco. She recently became the owner of Turquoise, a café bar in Cihangir on Istanbul's European side of the Bosporus, a neighborhood of bookshops and antique markets.

"Come for a visit," she wrote. "I want to show you the café."

Her transformation has left me flirting with regret that I, too, could have moved to Istanbul and started a new life.

When Joy calls to say that Bekir has invited us to Kalkan to meet his new wife, Pamela, I mention Kate's e-mail.

"What do you say?" says Joy. "Imagine flying to Istanbul with no agenda except to see our friends. Or to watch the freighters move through the Bosporus."

In early October, we awaken in Istanbul to a ripe, peach-colored sun rising over the Maiden's Tower near the Asian side of the Bosporus Strait. And we awaken to myth:

Once there was a sultan who had a beautiful daughter, whom he loved beyond measure. On the day she was born, the sultan and his wife summoned an oracle to predict the baby's future.

"Wise sultan, I have bad news," said the oracle. "If you are not vigilant, on your blessed daughter's eighteenth birthday, she will be bitten and killed by a snake."

When the girl's eighteenth birthday drew near, the sultan came up with a solution. In the deep blue water of the Bosporus near the Sea of Marmara, he built a tower. The girl lived at the very top in a circular room of pink marble embellished with silk and silver brocade, filled with storybooks illuminated in lapis lazuli and gold by the sultan's artists. During the day, she watched ships gliding into the Sea of Marmara, and at night, she was comforted by the distant lights of the palace.

On the morning of her eighteenth birthday, she rose and smiled. Tomorrow she would be free.

The eager sultan gathered gifts: a gold chain holding the key to his daughter's room, a dress of fine lavender brocade, and a basket made of reeds from the Tigris River and filled with sweet cherries from Giresun Province.

The delighted maiden put on her new dress and necklace and wove her long, tawny hair into a bun at the nape of her neck. Radiant, she joined her beloved father on a cushion to eat the sweet red fruit.

"After you, my precious daughter," said the sultan.

Filled with desire, the girl reached into the basket and touched a glistening cherry. She felt something slither through her fingers and slide up her arm. She screamed. A pale green asp, his eyes dark as basalt, aimed for her throat. He bared his fangs. The venom found its mark.

A Russian oil tanker's horn lets out a long, low warning as it moves past the Maiden's Tower toward Topkapı Palace. Did the venom *kill* the princess, I wonder, or did she fall into a trance?

From my cell phone, I dial the number for Kate's restaurant, Turquoise.

"Angie!" Kate shouts over the din of customers when I reach her at the bar. "I'm here for the evening. Come on over."

Joy and I navigate cobbled streets of Cihangir in curves and angles that delight as much as confuse us. Outside a used bookstore, Joy thumbs through a stack of old paperbacks, pulling Dashiell Hammett's *The Maltese Falcon* from a pile. Its cover displays the pale, curved back of a half-dressed woman and the silhouette of a man holding a red stiletto. Stamped inside the frontispiece are a Greek name and a Beyoğlu address.

I lose myself in a bin of black-and-white photos next to the paperbacks and sift through images of long-gone merchants of Beyoğlu in topcoats and fedoras, children in satin party dresses, women in tailored bouclé suits—memories of birthdays, graduations, and weddings cast off and sold to strangers for a few Turkish liras.

In a small courtyard beside a mosque, a blind man sleeps in a plastic chair, legs outstretched, chin pressed to his chest. Twice we try to find our way out of the neighborhood only to come upon him again.

Finally, at the corner of a busy intersection, Joy sees a sign displaying the word TURQUOISE and painted in a rich, elegant shade of blue. Open windows connect the diners inside with the convivial crowd on the street. Not so long ago, our clothes and hair would reek from smoke-filled haunts across Turkey. Now smoking is banned inside restaurants and bars, and smoke rises in curls and tendrils from the outdoor tables.

Near the entrance, a woman sits with a friend who holds an ivory holder containing a long, thin cigarette. The woman wears a knee-length, pleated black skirt, cropped sweater, plaid knee-highs, and high-heeled, pointy-toed pumps. I smile, thinking about how silly the outfit would look on my five-foot frame, while Joy takes notes for her next shopping trip to New York City.

"Merhaba. You made it!" Kate calls from behind the bar when we enter the café.

In a loose-knit taupe sweater draped slightly off one shoulder, she brushes dark bangs from a delicate face set off by black, rectangular glasses and rushes over for cheek kisses and hugs.

"Come. Sit here," she says.

Holding a fistful of receipts, she ushers us to a table by the window. "I have to get the day's receipts to my accountant. It won't take long, and by then my friend Hasan will be here. I've ordered rakı for you. Hope that's OK."

She disappears onto the street, her iPhone pressed to one ear. A waiter arrives with drinks, his hair slicked back to highlight eyes the color of pale green silk. The café cat, a white and cream calico, finds Joy's lap and purrs contentedly as we sip our drinks and observe the clientele, who range in age from midtwenties to eighties.

A few minutes later, Kate returns, carrying a bag with two bottles of Hennessy cognac.

"I have a customer, a writer, who works here in the afternoons, and this is what he likes to drink," she explains, handing the bag to one of her waiters.

Soon we're immersed in conversation and memories of Kalkan.

Joy mentions that we've lost touch with Wendy. "Although I still hope I'll run into her on a street corner someday," she says wistfully.

"I haven't heard from her, either," says Kate, "although a friend of mine, a travel writer, says she's still running her tour business in Greece and Turkey."

"You never know what fate might bring," says Joy.

When Kate asks if I've heard from Habib, I explain that while I haven't spoken to him in years, his niece Ebru has kept me up to date.

"Last fall, he was diagnosed with throat cancer," I say, as Kate eyes the pack of Marlboros she's set on the table. "He's in remission now, but Ayşe has devoted herself to caring for him in their Cappadocia house. Ebru says he plays cards all day and still drinks rakı at night."

"I always liked Habib," muses Kate. "But I remember how fond he was of his rakı.

"He could drink us all under the table," smiles Joy.

"No doubt he would have been difficult to live with," I say. "But I can't think of anyone who made me laugh more than he did."

"Didn't you two have a pact that when you turn seventy and if you are single, you would marry?" smiles Joy.

"He'll have to clear it with Ayşe now," I laugh, but I still feel a bittersweet pang.

A man of about twenty-five in straight-leg jeans, tight white T-shirt, and a black blazer calls Kate's name.

She motions him to sit next to her. "Hasan's specialty is *harabat*," she says when he sets down a music case containing a *saz*, a small stringed instrument. "You could say harabat is Turkish blues."

Sliding an arm across Kate's shoulders, Hasan engages her in an obviously flirtatious conversation in rapid-fire Turkish. Although it's clear that they are only friends, I'm reminded that regardless of age, men and women retain a playful sexuality within platonic friendships.

He asks if we've been to the Istanbul Modern Museum and if we know the photographs of Ara Güler, and nods in agreement when we observe that Güler's use of shadow and light and his ability to capture the mood of mid-twentieth-century Istanbul, especially the working class, have influenced how we see the city.

Our mutual admiration of Güler loosens any reserve Hasan might have had about us, and soon we're discussing politics and Turkey's bid to join the European Union.

"You cannot imagine all the requirements, regulations, and laws we would have to change if we are part of the EU," he says. "We've made many changes, especially in the area of human rights. But I honestly don't think Turkey needs the European Union."

"I'm not so sure Turkey should join the EU either," says Kate.

"Besides, we have everything we need," continues Hasan. "We already control most of the water that flows into the Middle East and can easily produce our own food. I believe water will become Turkey's political leverage for our future. So you see we don't need Europe. Maybe they need us more."

He checks his watch, gets up, and slings his saz over his shoulders. "I will play with some friends tonight at a club off Istiklal," he says, sharing hugs and cheek kisses. "Kate knows where to find me if you wish to come by."

"He's lovely," says Joy, after Hasan leaves. "Next time I should bring my daughter."

"Yes," says Kate, "you have to admit that young Turkish men are so appealing." She looks pointedly at me. "What are you waiting for, Angie? You should move to Istanbul. Maybe I'm being selfish, but you would fit in with our group of friends. Apartments in this neighborhood have become expensive, but another expat friend shares a flat across the Galata Bridge, in Balat. It's a more conservative area, but it's cheap, and the streets and markets remind me of Istanbul twenty years ago."

She scribbles the address of her real-estate broker and hands the slip of paper to me.

Joy raises an eyebrow and continues to pet the cat.

I put the slip of paper in my purse and try to imagine how I would keep up with Kate. I've spent the last ten years in the mountains among the oaks and coyotes, while Kate is used to urban life, having spent most of hers in San Francisco. Besides, I remind myself, I like straddling continents and lifestyles.

Later, lost in our own thoughts, Joy and I walk toward our hotel, past darkened shops and apartments where lights flicker behind drawn curtains and stray cats scrounge through bits of street trash or sleep on top of parked cars.

"I'm still sorry our house deal fell through in Cappadocia," she finally says. An orange tabby stares at her, its gold eyes reflecting the streetlights. "Truth is, even though I love my family, now that Sarah is in college and has her own apartment, I often think of settling here for a few months each year to research and write."

"The longing to live in both worlds," I say, echoing her thoughts.

Bosporus blue light has given way to the diaphanous pearly mist of the Aegean countryside. We are on our way from Istanbul to Kalkan, but since Joy has never been to Ephesus, we are making a pilgrimage.

Sprawled on cushions on the rooftop restaurant of our hotel in Selçuk, near the ruins of Ephesus, we drink coffee and savor the antics of a pair of black-and-white cats. They leap from a cinderblock wall in fruitless pursuit of a rose-colored canary, which taunts them from the safety of her cage beneath the eaves.

The sweet air hints at a sensuous unseen world of the feminine. In the east, remnants of the Anatolian mother goddess were hidden in caves, obscured in myth, and buried under monasteries and mosques. In Ephesus, however, excavations continue within several acres of marble, rubble, and dirt to reveal the high status of the Anatolian goddess the Ephesians called Artemis.

After breakfast, we walk to the Selçuk Museum to see the statue of Artemis. In the doorway of a timber and white-stucco house, two women tie herbs into bunches and place them into a wicker basket.

Tourist season has ended, and in the first gallery of the deserted museum, the god Priapus greets us. Naked and grinning, he shows off an erect phallus that balances a basket overflowing with grapes, apples, peaches, and pears. Protector of sailors, gardens, and grapes, he dares us, with a wicked grin, to admire his physical gift, a symbol of passion and fertility.

Artemis waits nearby in her own gallery. Upon her head rests an elaborate crown holding up a porticoed temple, representing the physical world ascending to Heaven. Signs of the zodiac circle her neck and tell the story of her connection to the stars and the mysteries they reveal. Like the mother goddess Cybele, to whom she is related, a lion rests on each arm, leaning protectively into her shoulders. Carved egg-shaped globes drape in rows of necklaces to her waist, above a tapered skirt decorated with bees and winged bulls.

Until recently, archaeologists and scholars thought the globes were breasts or eggs and that they represented fertility. A new generation of scholars says they are testicles, a symbol of male fertility willingly offered to Artemis in the endless cycle of sex, death, and rebirth.

The day has grown warm, and we shed our sweaters for the mile walk from Selçuk to the excavated city of Ephesus, once one of the busiest trading ports in the eastern Mediterranean. Each spring, the citizens of Ephesus celebrated the goddess with a festival called the Artemisia, during which traders, merchants, pilgrims, fakirs, and magicians crowded the road toward Ephesus to celebrate and honor the goddess. And of course, not unlike souvenir and food vendors at today's festivals, they attended the Artemisia to cash in on the spectacle.

On the Arcadiane, a thirty-five-foot-wide street of marble that once led to the harbor, we find the original public toilets. Instead of individual stalls, the room is lined with rows of marble seats that would have faced a tiled pool and a fountain of splashing marble dolphins.

"Almost makes it worth sitting with twenty other people and asking them to pass the water bucket," says Joy.

South of the public toilets, a footprint and heart carved into marble mark what the Turkish description calls *Aşkevi*, or Love House, better known as the city's brothel, where an open greeting room surrounds small cubicles outfitted with stone beds.

"Can you imagine such a place right out here in the marketplace?" says a heavyset woman with champagne-colored curls. She wears a lime-green T-shirt identifying the cruise ship from which she and a group of fellow travelers have disembarked. Emblazoned across her back in gold are words that remind us to "Start the Day the Lord's Way."

The men take turns placing Teva-clad feet inside the footprint while their wives shake their heads in equal amounts of disgust and amusement.

"Take our picture," a tall, thin, balding man calls to his wife.

She snaps the picture and mutters, "No wonder the apostle Paul wanted to shut down the city."

Paul spent two years in Ephesus, the longest he lived anywhere during his missionary years. Like Antioch, Ephesus was a perfect place for Paul to spread the word of a new savior, Jesus Christ. The residents of Ephesus, a cosmopolitan trading center, tolerated competing faiths and evangelists who preached their Good News from every street corner.

Fitting easily into the milieu, winning converts among Jewish and pagan citizens alike, Paul spoke of a single God and His son, Jesus Christ, a divine man born of a virgin, a man who died so all who believed in his unseen Father would gain eternal life and whose message surpassed that of all the gods and goddesses who came before him.

Paul had planned to leave in Ephesus after the Artemisia festival, where he would convert pilgrims arriving from throughout the Aegean and Mediterranean worlds. But a silversmith named Demetrios, who made and sold icons of the goddess, heard Paul preach against worshipping false images echoing the words of the Prophet Abraham: "Gods made by human hands are not gods at all."

Fearing he would lose his livelihood, Demetrios gathered his fellow workmen, warning them not only that they would lose their businesses, but also that their goddess had been discredited.

An angry Demetrios and his fellow workmen mounted a protest, marching through the streets and shouting, "Great is Artemis of the Ephesians!" People heard their shouts and took up the chant. Thousands filled the theater. The crowd grew violent, and a riot broke out.

When the town clerk was summoned, he threatened the protesters with fines and imprisonment. The crowd dispersed, but Paul, fearing that he would be murdered, left for less hostile territory in Macedonia.

Paul's words would eventually silence the goddess. In 312 CE, the Roman Emperor Constantine accepted Christianity and ordered all images of gods and goddesses to be removed from sanctuaries.

Near Ephesus, a house made of stone stands on a shaded hill. Tradition says that Meryemana, the Blessed Virgin Mary, spent the final years of her life here and died in Ephesus. We join the Christian cruise-goers and a group of Muslim women making the pilgrimage up the hill to Mary's house.

To thousands of pilgrims, it makes no difference that the house was built three centuries after Mary's death. Or that it wasn't discovered until the nineteenth century, when Anne Catherine Emmerich, a bedridden German woman who had never visited Turkey, saw it in a vision.

Inspired by Emmerich's description of a dwelling constructed of stone blocks with rounded arches, a priest from the nearby port city of Izmir traveled to Ephesus and found an abandoned house nestled in a pine grove overlooking the Aegean.

Following a tradition stretching back to their nomadic and shamanistic past, worshippers tie white strips of cloth to a tree near the house so their prayers may be answered.

"Let's add our own prayers for our journey to Kalkan," suggests Joy, searching through her backpack for anything we might use to tie into wishes.

An older woman wearing an embroidered scarf, lines etched at her mouth and the corners of her sea-blue eyes, has been watching us. She tears two small strips from a piece of loosely woven fabric and presses one in each of our palms.

"*Adak Adamak*," she says, "for an offering."

Joy finds space on one of the upper branches, while I squeeze next to the older woman and find room on a lower branch.

I tie the fabric with three knots, one for Joy, one for me, and one for our journey to Kalkan.

An hour before sunset, we tentatively disembark under the Kâmil Koç sign on Kalkan's main road above the harbor. Humid air envelops us with a mother's warmth. In a flash, time stops.

"Is that the same nut vendor?" says Joy, pointing to a familiar cart next to the post office.

"I think so," I say, but I'm somewhere else, half believing Habib is waiting for me in the harbor at Lipsos Bar, even though Nusrat closed it years ago.

"Oh, my friends, I cannot believe I am seeing you with my own two eyes," Bekir says later, as we settle into the Yalı Bar in the center of Kalkan. From the enthusiastic bear hugs and kisses he bestows, any lingering thought that our homecoming might be uncomfortable vanishes.

"Pamela is in Antalya tonight and will be back tomorrow," he adds. "She's eager to meet you."

Bekir's romantic nature and generosity often got in the way of good business sense until he met Pamela, who eventually quit her marketing job in London and has since cleaned the dust off Bekir's antique shop. Together, they've built one of Kalkan's most successful real-estate agencies.

"We will have a barbecue at our house tomorrow night," he says.

When I mention the increased number of houses on the hillside above Kalkan, he grins. "Yes, business is very good."

From large corner speakers, a deep, syncopated beat fills the bar, giving way to the hit song "Şımarık"—"Spoiled"—by Tarkan, Turkey's version of Justin Timberlake.

Bekir lifts his arms, rolls one shoulder and then the other, offers Joy his hand, and leads her to the dance floor. I sip my rakı and munch on carrot and cucumber sticks soaking in a glass of salted lemon water.

Doğan, my friend and former suitor who still owns his silver shop, pulls up a chair and shares that he's now married to a German woman with whom he has a three-year-old son.

"It is difficult, but we make it work," he says, explaining that she and his son spend the school year in Berlin.

"Do you remember the silver and leather flask you bought for too many liras in the Grand Bazaar?" he says, breaking into laughter. "We filled it with rakı and it immediately began to leak, so you asked if I would solder it shut."

"All too well," I say.

"When I put my torch to the flask, I saw it wasn't made of silver at all. It was plastic coated with silver paint." Again he breaks into a hearty laugh, causing Joy and Bekir to return to the table. Bekir picks up the story.

"You turned a tiny pinhole into a hole the size of my thumb," Bekir says, raising a thick digit.

"Yes," says Doğan, waving a carrot stick at me. "I am a silversmith and should have known better."

"But there was no problem," says Bekir. "You are still the best silversmith in all of Turkey. Remember, I turned the flask upside down, put a rose in the hole, and set it on the fireplace mantel at The Ruins? It stayed there until I moved and married Pamela."

The DJ plays a tango, and we all take to the dance floor as if we never left.

Pamela's Renault climbs toward the ridge above town, toward her and Bekir's villa, tucked into the mountainside and overlooking the sea.

"Don't hit my chicken!" Bekir says as a fat, tawny-red rooster flaps up on a rock and lets out a squawk.

Pamela keeps a steady uphill momentum on the last switchback to the villa. "I think you love your chickens more than me," she says.

Bekir smiles and kisses her cheek.

"He only wants to raise chickens and goats," she says.

"I warned you that I am just a village man," says Bekir, cheerfully.

"I didn't *marry* a village man," Pamela says with a good-natured sigh.

Their villa speaks more to Zen modern than a house in a rustic village. Mosaic glass tiles in ochre and jade green are embedded into an arched doorway from which one of Bekir's engraved lanterns hangs. Inside, pale gray walls anchor Bekir's collection of kilims and carpets. A brass pitcher, an oil lamp, Roman glass, and an antique censor are displayed in niches. Windows open to a stone patio overlooking the whitewashed and stone buildings of Kalkan and a platinum-blue bay.

My heart aches and I think back to my first evening in Kalkan, when I had expected to find Orhan waiting at the bus station.

"From Wendy's descriptions, this is what I thought the Sun Pension would have looked like," says Joy, as if reading my mind.

Bekir prepares lamb shish kebab for the grill while Joy chops mint and I dice cucumbers for the yogurt-and-mint cacık that will accompany it.

Pamela plugs in her iPod, and the heady notes of the flutelike ney lift into the air and swirl around us.

When the sun drops into the sea, tawny red as the rooster's feathers, and we've toasted Bekir and Pamela with glasses of rakı, Bekir asks, "Have you been back to the pension?"

"Not yet," says Joy.

"You won't believe it," he says. "I think it will not be standing much longer. You must see it again with your own eyes."

The following evening, just before cocktail hour, we walk in sunlight and shadow, past carpet shops and pottery shops and glass shops and a store selling Turkish delight below a second-floor flat, where I remember an old woman with thin, wispy hair peeking from an embroidered headscarf lowering a wicker basket tied to a rope. The basket contained her rust-and-white, short-haired French terrier, and when the basket reached the ground, the terrier would leap out and take himself for a walk.

Near what was once Lipsos Bar, another abandoned house is being renovated, its kitchen garden filled with fennel and dill gone to seed and waving golden-brown heads.

"Maybe the Sun Pension *is* already gone," says Joy. "Shouldn't it be here?"

Our instinct tells us to turn left along a stone path between a row of houses.

"Stop," I say when we reach the harbor. "There's the mansion."

Oiled mahogany window frames shine against whitewashed plaster. An elegant pine door carved in arabesques guards an entryway, waiting for its once and future captain to trudge home from faraway ports. Beyond the gate, a fountain splashes droplets of water on a basalt and marble-tiled patio.

The small grocery store at the corner is gone, replaced by a modern two-story apartment building with balconies turned toward the sea.

We see the pension at the same time. Leaning toward the modern apartment building like a frail old man who refuses to die.

The bougainvillea that redeemed the pension from its flaws has been cut back to only a few twisting vines, revealing the sagging balcony and cracked and broken windows. The back steps have no railing at all. We climb them, bracing our palms against the house to avoid falling through rotting wood.

Afraid to disturb lingering ghosts, Joy gingerly knocks on the door. When no one answers, she pushes the door open, and we tiptoe into the lobby. The desk is gone. The kitchen cupboards are bare, and it quickly becomes clear that even ghosts have abandoned this place. Inside my old room, vines have grown through window frames, twining across a single stained mattress propped against the wall.

"Come out here," Joy calls from the balcony.

Without its harbor view, the balcony is simply a shabby buffer for the apartment across the way. We can easily lean over the scarred railing and touch a sleek glass window where partially open eyelet curtains reveal a modern kitchen with a granite counter and dishes drying in a rack next to a stainless steel sink.

A table is pushed against the pension's cedar facade. Chipped and faded blue chairs are stacked on top, their rush seating as disheveled as a bird's nest invaded by a crow. Although it's impossible to sit on the chairs, we remove them from the table so Joy can set down her backpack. She unzips it and withdraws a bottle of white Çannakale wine, a corkscrew, and two plastic glasses.

Twisting the corkscrew into the cork, she pulls it out with a pop, and pours the pale yellow wine into the glasses. Lifting them she offers one to me.

We sit cross-legged in silence on the splintery floorboards and take a sip. My thoughts return to the days when the village dog, Priscilla, a scraggly blond mutt, would climb the stairs on hot afternoons, stretch out on the porch, and fall asleep. I remember the anticipation of an evening at Lipsos. How the mind plays tricks by forgetting the nasty looks from Orhan and the long, hot nights when I needed earplugs to drown out the drone of mosquitoes.

"Şerefe," Joy finally says, touching her glass to mine.

We watch the sea flow into Kalkan Harbor, where through the ages a hundred languages have been spoken, where the muezzin's call has replaced church bells, where evangelists, travelers, entrepreneurs, farmers, adventurers, and dreamers like us have left a part of themselves within this golden fold of mountain.

"So, *Melek*," says Joy, using my Turkish name. "Tell me the truth. Are you finished with Turkey?"

EPILOGUE

We sit on the stone ledge beside the girl's gift, olives from trees whose roots have spread toward the sea for a thousand years. She watches us from the shelter of the pines.

"Merhaba," we call, and smile.

She hesitates before shyly stepping into sunlight.

The water glints like sapphires.

"Merhaba," she says. "Hello."

ACKNOWLEDGMENTS

We are blessed to have had the opportunity to experience the many wonders and hospitality of Turkey and her people. Gratitude to our Muslim, Alevi, Zoroastrian, Sufi, Kurdish, Jewish, Christian, Greek, Syrian, Armenian, and Arab friends and acquaintances who showed us their country's diversity. And to the many kind strangers who accepted us into their lives and gave us a place to stay.

We thank: Şakir Karaaslan, who introduced us to his family and taught us how to shop for spices; Bridget Karaaslan for sharing her husband with us; Namik Safyürek, who gave us our Turkish names—Melek, "Angel," and Sevinc, "Joy"; Kemal and Patty Safyürek, who showed us ancient Lycia; Hasan Semerci and Murat Küpçü, who, to paraphrase poet William Blake, taught us to "see the world in a carpet"; Levent Demirel, former director of the Turkish National Tourist Office in New York, who embraced our vision for this book; Ali Akşar, who showed us the nightlife in Cihangir; Shellie Corman and Dany Vallerand, who were part of the journey; Necat Agirman and Faruk for taking good care of us on the Black Sea; Mustafa Özdemir and Gabriel Oktay Çilli for their friendship in the Southeast; Friends who inspired us were: Erguvan Toplu, Halit Teker, Attile Artuner, Tunç Cebe, Eveline Zoutendjik, Rosemary Carstens, Nebahat Akkoç, and all the brave women at KAMER in Diyarbakır.

Angie thanks the staff and students at Spencer Valley School; the Julian Library Board; the members of her Julian book group; and friends and family in Oregon and beyond for their time, patience, and moral support. A big thanks to independent bookseller Melony Vance, who gave her support from the very first draft.

Joy thanks: her parents, Peter and Dorothy Stocke, and her extended family, especially sister Amy Constantine; The New York Public Library, in whose Oriental Studies Reading Room the early chapters of this book were written; poet and cultural philosopher William Irwin Thompson, whose symposia at the Cathedral of Saint John the Divine in New York City inspired the journey. She thanks the following friends and colleagues who often put aside their own work to read and critique the manuscript: Elizabeth Bako, Fran Metzman, Dennis O'Donnell, Raquel B. Pidal, Katherine Schimmel, Joann Young, and the staff of the online magazine *Wild River Review*, where a number of chapters were edited and published—especially Executive Editor Kim Nagy for her patience and excellent edits.

We are indebted to: Anne Mery and Susan McMillion for invaluable critiques from a woman's point of view; Humerya Konak and Alev Yalman for their careful, thoughtful edits and feedback on language and content; Melek Pulatkonak, founder of Turkish Women's International Network; Dan Gordon, editor extraordinaire; The Blue House in Istanbul and the Kelebek in Cappadocia, where we wrote portions of this book. A huge hug to Joy's husband, Fred Young, for putting up with her numerous trips to Turkey and California and for leaving us alone during endless hours in New Jersey with our laptops, interrupting only to bring tea or glasses of wine/rakı when the workday extended into the evening.

Finally, we thank our friend Wendy—traveler, businesswoman, entrepreneur—who brought us together. May we meet again on a far-flung shore.

BIBLIOGRAPHY

Balakian, Peter. *The Burning Tigris*. William Heinemann, 2002.

Bean, George E. *Aegean Turkey*. London: John Murray, 1989.

———. *Turkey's Southern Shore*. London: John Murray, 1968.

Bible, King James Version. Cleveland, Ohio: World Publishing Company, 1956.

Blake, Everett C. *Biblical Sites in Turkey*. Istanbul: Redhouse, 1977.

Caesar, E. Farah. *Islam*, Fifth Edition. Hauppauge, New York: Barrons, 1994.

Cilingirolu, Altan. *The History of the Kingdom of Van, Urartu*. Izmir, Turkey: Ofis Ticaret Matbaacilik, 2000.

Cimok, Fatih. *A Guide to the Seven Churches*. Istanbul: A Turizm Yayinlari, 1998.

———. *Antioch on the Orontes*. Istanbul: A Turizm Yayinlari, 1994.

Dubin, Marc S., and Lucas Envers. *Trekking in Turkey*. Victoria, Australia: Lonely Planet Publications, 1989.

Edmonds, Anna C. *Biblical Sites in Turkey*. Istanbul: Redhouse, 1977.

Freely, John. *Classical Turkey, Architectural Guides of Travellers*. London: Penguin Books, 1990.

Goodwin, Jason. *Lords of the Horizons: A History of the Ottoman Empire*. New York: Henry Holt, 1998.

Güler, Ara. *A Photographical Sketch on Lost Istanbul*. Istanbul: Dunya Siketler Grubu, 1994.

Halo, Thea. *Not Even My Name*. New York: Picador USA, 2000.

Kelly, Laurence. *Istanbul, a Travellers' Companion*. New York: Atheneum, 1987.

Kinross, Lord. *Atatürk: The Rebirth of a Nation*. Northern Cyprus: K. Rustem & Brothers, 1964.

———. *The Ottoman Centuries: The Rise and Fall of the Turkish Empire*. New York: Morrow Quill Paperback, 1977.

Kinzer, Stephen. *Crescent & Star.* New York: Farrar, Strauss and Giroux, 2002.

Lewis, Bernard. *The Emergence of Modern Turkey.* New York: Oxford University Press, 2002.

Lewis, Raphaela. *Everyday Life in Ottoman Turkey.* New York: Dorset Press, 1971.

Macaulay, Rose. *The Towers of Trebizond.* London: Collins, 1956.

Mango, Andrew. *Atatürk: Biography of the Founder of Modern Turkey.* Woodstock & New York: Overlook, 1999.

Mansel, Phillip. *Constantinople: City of the World's Desire, 1453–1924.* New York: St. Martin's Griffin, 1998.

Mantran, Robert. *Turkey.* New York: The Viking Press, 1959.

McDonagh, Bernard. *Blue Guide Turkey.* London: A&C Black; and New York: WW Norton, 1995.

Morton, H. V. *In the Steps of St. Paul.* Cambridge, Massachusetts: Da Capo, 2002.

Neumann, Erich. *The Great Mother.* Bollingen Series XLVII. New York: Pantheon, 1963.

Önen, Ülgür. *Lycia, Western Section of the Southern Anatolian Coast.* Izmir: Duyal Matbaacilik Sanayi, 1984.

Özgür, M. Edip. *Aspendos.* Istanbul: Net Turistik Yayinlar, 1988.

Pope, Nicole and Hugh. *Turkey Unveiled: A History of Modern Turkey.* Woodstock & New York: Overlook, 1997.

Rubin, Barry. *Istanbul Intrigues: Espionage, Sabotage, and Diplomatic Treachery in the Spy Capital of WWII.* New York: Pharos Books, 1991.

Rüstemolu, Jale. *Antioch, Mosaic Pavement.* Antakya, Turkey: Zirem Yayinlari, 1997.

Schimmel, Annemarie. *The Triumphal Sun.* Persian Studies Series. Albany, New York: State University of New York Press, 1993.

Settle, Mary Lee. *Turkish Reflections: A Biography of a Place.* New York: Touchstone, 1992.

Stark, Freya. *Alexander's Path.* New York: The Overlook Press, 1988.

———. *The Lycian Shore.* New York: Harcourt, Brace and Company, 1956.

Stoneman, Richard. *A Traveller's History of Turkey.* New York: Interlink Books, 1998.

Tülek, Füsun. *Orpheus, the Magician*. Istanbul: Arkeoloji Ve Sanat Yayinlari, 1998.

Wallach, Janet. *Desert Queen: The Extraordinary Life of Gertrude Bell*. New York: Anchor, 1999.

Wheatcroft, Andrew. *The Ottomans: Dissolving Images*. London: Penguin Books, 1993.

Yale, Pat, Verity Campbell, and Richard Plunkett. *Lonely Planet, Turkey*. Victoria, Australia: Lonely Planet Publications, 2003.

ABOUT THE AUTHORS

Joy E. Stocke, left, and Angie Brenner at Hasankeyf, Turkey

ANGIE BRENNER began her love affair with Turkey when she embarked on a quest to see Whirling Dervishes in Konya, where Sufi mystic Jelaluddin Rumi taught. An avid traveler and illustrator, Brenner would spend the next twenty-five years searching the remote corners of Turkey for historical and cultural links between Turkey's past and present. A freelance writer and former bookstore owner, Brenner is the West Coast Editor for the online magazine *Wild River Review*. She lives in the rural mountain community of Julian, California.

JOY E. STOCKE has been traveling to and writing about Turkey and the eastern Aegean since 1982. Her quest to discover the roots of Western religion has brought her to all of Turkey's borders. She is the author of a novel, *Ugly Cookies*, and a collection of bilingual poems (English/Greek), *The Cave of the Bear*, based on her travels in Crete. Founder and Editor-In-Chief of the online magazine *Wild River Review*, Stocke is a Lindisfarne Association fellow and serves on the board of the Princeton Middle East Society. She lives in Stockton, New Jersey.